Notes from the Caroline Underground

STUDIES IN BRITISH HISTORY AND CULTURE

VOLUME VI

Notes from the Caroline Underground

Alexander Leighton, the Puritan Triumvirate,
and the
Laudian Reaction to Nonconformity

by
STEPHEN FOSTER

Published for
The Conference on British Studies and Wittenberg University
by ARCHON BOOKS

Library of Congress Cataloging in Publication Data

Foster, Stephen, 1942-
    Notes from the Caroline underground.

    (Studies in British history and culture; v. 6)
    Bibliography: p.
    Includes index.
    1. Leighton, Alexander, 1568-1649. 2. Puritans—Eng-
land—History. 3. England—Church history—17th century.
4. Persecution—England. 5. Laud, William, Abp. of
Canterbury, 1573-1645. I. Title. II. Series.
BX9339.L4F67   285′.9′0922   78-9595
ISBN 0-208-01758-5

First published 1978 as an Archon Book,
an imprint of The Shoe String Press, Inc.,
Hamden, Connecticut
for
The Conference on British Studies
and
Wittenberg University
Springfield, Ohio

75230

Printed in the United States of America

FOR VERNA

CONTENTS

FOREWORD

Studies in British History and Culture was founded in January, 1965, as a joint publishing venture of the Conference on British Studies and the University of Bridgeport; Stephen Graubard and Leland Miles were the Senior Editors, and the New York University Press was printer. Three volumes were published in the series under this arrangement, the last being in 1970. A five year hiatus then occurred when the University of Bridgeport decided that it could no longer fund the series. Fortunately, Wittenberg University volunteered to become co-publisher with the conference and with Archon Books. Since that time the series has published two books.

The intention of the conference and the editors in establishing the monograph series was to publish works of vigorous research, original interpretation, and literary grace which fell between the regular article and the full length book. The editors were especially seeking works which would challenge traditional viewpoints or advance new theses and works which would integrate particular events with larger themes.

In this sixth volume of the series, Stephen Foster argues that the Caroline underground was much less well organized than many people have thought. Censorship was sufficiently effective to make clandestine printing in England itself almost impossible. Works were often printed in Amsterdam and then smuggled into the country. At that point the tracts had to be circulated; but the distribution system was so primitive that many copies fell into the hands of the government, together with the amateur dealers themselves. Government then, and students later, thought that they were dealing with a phenomenon of great size; but this iceberg had no submerged seven-eighths. Laud was fooled into thinking he saw a conspiracy where nothing worthy of the name existed. He came to fear that the conspiracy threatened his life. And by his increasingly vigorous attempts at repression he managed, in time, to bring about his own death. Rarely has a self-fulfilling prophecy worked out so neatly. Leighton, the first of the martyrs, had little or nothing to do with Burton or Bastwick or Prynne. By mutilating them all, Laud so embittered the tone of the political dialogue that he may be said to have created the Revolution. This is a thesis which will certainly make for discussion.

Stephen Baxter
Leland Miles
Senior Editors

PREFACE

IF, LIKE SOME PURITAN SERMON, this monograph were to begin by
"opening" a text, the passage chosen would come from a paper
delivered by Patrick Collinson in 1966:

> The progressive protestant cause in Elizabethan England
> can be compared to a tripod, consisting of puritan preachers,
> adherents and sympathisers among the nobility and gentry,
> and the popular element which contemporaries normally had
> in mind when they spoke substantively of "the godly" . . .
> Clerical puritanism is the most adequately explored: for "pu-
> ritan" in much of the literature, read "puritan minister." A
> more recent discovery has been the reliance of progressive
> protestanism on the patronage of the landed classes, a depen-
> dence less than that of the catholic recusant community, but
> probably the key to the fluctuations in its local and national
> fortunes. By comparison, the contribution of the lower orders
> remains an unknown quantity.

Collinson arguably overstated his strictures to make his point, and
the subsequent publication of his own *Elizabethan Puritan Move-*

ment has gone a long way towards recovering the role of the Puritan laity in the period prior to the Hampton Court conference of 1604. After this date, however, Collinson's "popular element" still inhabits an historiographic *terra incognita* whose rough boundaries are well enough known but whose interior territory is unexplored. On the one hand, the importance of the laity and of their exclusive private exercises is widely acknowledged; on the other, once this acknowledgement is made, studies of Jacobean and Caroline Puritanism generally return to the congenial business of explicating clerical discourse or classifying the nature and extent of clerical nonconformity.

This essay takes a different tack, attempting to discover something more of "the godly"—their activities, organization, and political potential—by examining the careers of four prominent Puritan polemicists who, with varying degrees of enthusiasm, became caught up in the lay-dominated world of conventicling and clandestine publishing. "The Caroline Underground" may seem a rather dramatic way to describe a series of disparate activities linked together mainly by an overlapping set of participants. Some one designation, however, is appropriate for widespread, relatively frequent lay meetings sufficiently similar to be classed together, although sufficiently informal and improvisatory to refute any attempt to categorize them under a more precise heading. And the word "underground" at least emphasizes the slightly raffish reputation its participants enjoyed within the Puritan movement as a whole, as well as the ever present possibility of their coming in conflict with the episcopal establishment and, consequently, the necessary obscurity of many of their activities.

Fortunately, considerable documentation does exist for the most spectacular of these furtive enterprises: the composition, publication, and circulation of antiepiscopal invectives, of which the best known are the works of my four protagonists, Alexander Leighton, John Bastwick, Henry Burton, and William Prynne. The subject is at once well-studied and underexploited, largely because of the regretable failure of two groups of scholars with common interests to appreciate the value of combining their respective techniques. Most bibliographers of the clandestine literature of the Jacobean and Caroline period approach their subject primarily through textual and typographic analysis of the apposite works, with comparatively little attention given to the historian's mainstay, the manuscript source. Most historians repay the compliment by regarding bibliographic inquiry as a mechanical necessity tangential to their main interests. For the bibliographer the consequence has been outright errors in the assignment of printers and occasionally of authors, as well as assertions based on improbable conjecture, while historians of Puritanism have, on the whole, found themselves admitting the central importance of personal connections to the movement and yet rarely taking more than an incidental interest in one of the few unambiguous pieces of evidence concerning these ties.

In a pioneering article in 1964 Marc Curtis demonstrated just how much could be learned by joining the historian's knowledge and concerns to the bibliographer's repertory. His study of the Puritan printer William Jones both corrected an earlier canon for an important Dutch press and brought into focus for the first time a radical group of Jacobean Puritans, who had hidden their anti-episcopal maneuvering so well the sole trace of their activity was a series of clandestine tracts. In turn, some of Curtis's major characters have minor roles to play in this study, where a similar combination of interests is essential to discover the ligaments of radical Puritan organization for the Caroline period and to uncover the dynamics of the interaction between laity and clergy, moderate and extremist.

The picture of Puritan politics that emerges is considerably more complex than previous accounts will allow. In particular, a reexamination of the printing and distribution of Puritan tracts reveals the growing cooperation after 1635 between the members of the Caroline underground and a far more respectable group of militants personified by Henry Burton and William Prynne. The formation of this peculiar alliance in turn estranged more cautious Puritan opinion in the crucial years before the Civil War, helping to lay the basis for the suspicions and animosities that issued in the great rupture of the 1640s.

William Lamont has offered a somewhat similar thesis in his intellectual biography of Prynne, and William Haller has written of the emergence of "populistic Puritanism" in the late 1630s, but both men present the phenomenon out of context. Haller neglects the long history of lay exercises and the degree of ministerial support they attracted, inaccurately assuming that these activities must be the work of anticlerical "tub preachers." Lamont similarly plays down Prynne's willingness to make common cause with the

Separatists and various other sectaries during his imprisonment in the Tower, making him a late convert to radicalism who was temporarily swept out of his normal moderation by the chiliastic expectations of the years 1640-42. Neither account of events is entirely in error, but both historians maintain a static, overrigid distinction between "mainline" Puritanism and the allegedly peripheral elements in the same movement because of their rather abstract notion of the immediate circumstances surrounding the publication of the works they explicate.

More disturbingly, another staple item in the historiography of the 1630s rests, as it turns out, on no very solid foundation: historians as diverse as Haller, H. R. Trevor-Roper, and S. R. Gardiner have all accepted Archbishop Laud's own assessment of the danger in which he stood as a result of Puritan propaganda, particularly as it mounted in intensity and vehemence after 1635. Such doubts as have crept in have merely taken the form of questioning whether persuasive rhetoric can really persuade. (Trevor-Roper, for one, speculates that most readers could not wade through Prynne's longer efforts.) The more fundamental question of just how many people this literature actually reached has gone unasked as well as unanswered, in Laud's day and in our own. Allowing for incomplete documentation, the surviving records invariably suggest that regardless of the power of the tract, few people had the opportunity of reading it besides its targets. In reality, the post-1635 "flood" of libels represented mainly a rise in the number of titles and not in their circulation.

The arguments in support of this conclusion, laid out in Chapter VII, may not convince every reader—much remains unknown and in some instances unknowable. Yet, whatever the final verdict, it is still necessary to confront the question of why Laud chose to undertake a policy of repression in the first place. He could, instead, have interpreted a large body of evidence, as available to him as to us, to mean that his enemies would never have attracted much attention unless he himself went to the trouble of providing them with an audience. Accidents of circumstance account in part for Laud's decision, but he was in any case peculiarly liable to decide as he did because of the assumptions about the volatility and hostility of "the people" that he shared in a highly unoriginal way with most of his contemporaries. Lack of originality is one characteristic rarely attributed to the archbishop, who has managed to retain the stature his enemies endowed him with as the would-be architect of revolutionary change. His efforts may be judged daring or foolhardy, grand or execrable, but in his ecclesiastical goals and political mission he usually comes off as the one man who dared to challenge the rules of the game inherited from the reigns of Elizabeth and James I.

This version of Laud's goals has been set down enough times in enough detail to stand in no great risk of total displacement. It may be an accurate judgment of his theology and ecclesiology, but in his ill-fated campaign against his more visible Puritan enemies, his views were unquestioningly, even unthinkingly traditional: his diagnosis rested on familiar notions of the many-headed monster and the reckless sectarian adventurers liable to inflame it, and he responded to the threat with routine countermeasures based on implicit faith in the salutary effect of exemplary punishment. Indeed, if Laud had been anything other than highly unoriginal on these points, the rest of the Star Chamber would hardly have joined with him in three major state trials that turned out to be serious political errors. As an historical figure, the archbishop quite possibly merits the fate that has overtaken his colleague Strafford; that is, demotion to the status of an intelligent and vigorous administrator of limited inventive powers, whose perfectly comprehensible mistakes of policy happened to have far-reaching consequences.

Throughout this monograph I have attempted to explain the actions taken by all sides in pretty much these same terms, as understandable responses to understandable problems. In the era of the Gunpowder Plot and the Overbury poisoning none of the protagonists needs to be written off as "paranoid." Rather, a surer way to approach both Laud and his opponents is with a sense of irony tempered by a degree of sympathy. For irony arises from a situation in which considered actions produce consequences directly opposite to those intended by the actors, and that is both a good summary of what follows and a description of a joke ultimately played upon us all.

Williamsburg, Va.   S.F.

ACKNOWLEDGEMENTS

IT IS SOMETHING of a commonplace that the debts an author accumulates in writing a work of scholarship can never really be repaid. They can at least be acknowledged.

The bulk of the research for this study was completed while I had the privilege of being a fellow of the John Simon Guggenheim Memorial Foundation and of enjoying a sabbatical leave from Northern Illinois University. A subsequent summer salary provided by my university enabled me to complete most of my work in English archives, and earlier grants-in-aid from the American Council of Learned Societies and the American Philosophical Society provided my first introduction to these collections. My interest in the trans-Atlantic aspects of Puritan culture and in what has come to be called popular Protestantism dates back earlier still, to 1968-69 when I held a younger scholar fellowship awarded by the National Endowment for the Humanities.

The degree to which this study concentrates on fugitive tracts and obscure authors and publishers indicates the extent to which I have depended on the good auspices of research libraries and their librarians. Mr. D. Pepys Whiteley of Magdalene College, Cambridge, kindly allowed me to see a rare tract of Alexander

Leighton's, and the Librarian of the Inner Temple Library was equally helpful in permitting me to consult a manuscript record of Leighton's Case. My demands, ordinary and extraordinary, on the services of the staffs of the British Library, the Public Record Office, the Bodleian Library, the Lambeth Palace Library, Dr. Williams's Library, the Guildhall Library, and the Newberry Library were met with unfailing courtesy and assistance.

At one time or another a remarkable number of individuals have read some draft or portion of this work. I should particularly like to thank for their efforts, criticisms, and encouragement Stephen Baxter, T. H. Breen, Verna Ann Foster, C. H. George, Albert A. Hayden, Caroline M. Hibbard, J. Sears McGee, Edmund S. Morgan, and Kenneth W. Shipps. I profited greatly during the course of my research from attending the seminar on seventeenth-century England held at the Institute of Historical Research, London, under the direction of R. W. Lockyer, H. G. Roseveare, and Ian Roy, and chapter six shows the influence of my experience with an earlier draft presented as a paper at the 1974 convention of the Rocky Mountain Conference on British Studies. Yeoman service in typing and retyping the manuscript was rendered by Deborah Gallagher and Elaine Kittelson. Finally, though they had no direct part in the present work, I should be very remiss in my duty if I did not mention my gratitude for the opportunity to study at Yale University while W. H. Dunham, Jr., and J. H. Hexter were members of the faculty.

I

THE SETTING

The Caroline Underground

WHEN THE LONG PARLIAMENT assembled in 1640 a general jail
delivery quickly set at liberty a heterogeneous collection of individuals who had suffered before Star Chamber or High Commission for their opposition to the episcopal establishment of the
Church of England. The group included, among others, the future
Leveller John Lilburne, the battered Separatist visionary Thomas
Brewer, the ultra-militant polemicist Alexander Leighton, and,
easily the most famous of all, the "Triumvirate" of 1637—William
Prynne, Henry Burton, and John Bastwick, released for a joyful
reunion in 1640, to be followed presently by a falling out no less
enthusiastic.

In retrospect these men may seem to have had little really in
common beyond their shared confinement, and during the next few
years they would indeed go their very separate ways. But in 1640
each had every reason to consider himself part of a single movement, and, in fact, at some point all of them had found themselves
willing participants in a kind of Puritan underground, an ecclesiastical half-world located outside the regular parish assemblies as
well as the outlawed congregations of the Separatists. Throughout
the reigns of James and Charles "godly" laity and their clerical

1

allies had come together irregularly but repeatedly for extra-parochial religious exercises, for the publication and distribution of clandestine literature, and, without too much regard for de-nominational niceties, for the aid and comfort of the Protestant enemies of episcopacy wherever they might be found. Thus, Thomas Brewer, a sectary of the sectaries, associate of the Pilgrims, and later patron of the Kentish Brownists, still took under his roof in 1617 two fellow countrymen newly arrived at Leyden, Alexander Leighton and John Bastwick, though both men emphatically rejected Separatism, and three years later in 1620 he offered the services of his short-lived press to the Scottish Presbyterians for their struggle against the bishops. So too William Prynne, the perennial odd man out of Puritan politics, who, nevertheless, in the midst of his imprisonment came to identify with Brewer and Leighton and (like others) to avail himself of the services of a network of Separatists and semi-Separatists for the publication of the increasingly extreme tracts he was composing in the Tower.[1]

This style of Puritanism resists both easy classification and complete reconstruction. Its very existence depended on the casual association of men of differing opinions whose shadowy activities were only occasionally illuminated by the unwelcome glare of informers' reports and High Commission proceedings. To the episcopal authorities, who caught sight of them only in snatches, coincidence could seem conspiracy, intermittent contact an organized "presbytery," until the personal safety of the bishops no less than the salvation of the English church as by law established was held to depend on firmer and firmer measures. "But here is no 'thorough,' and that's the bane of all," Archbisop Laud would complain in 1637 after the trial of Burton, Bastwick, and Prynne had failed to reduce their "brethern" to obedience or at least to sullen quiescence. Laud's episcopal rival, the devious but astute John Williams, correctly judged "the killing and massacring of these poore flies" to be both unwarranted and self-defeating, but Laud's fatal misjudgment was not completely implausible.[2] Rarely glimpsing the world of the radicals except when one of its members was apprehended writing, printing, or distributing seditious litera-ture, he realized neither the true extent of such activities nor their limitations, and he exaggerated both the appeal of the more ex-treme forms of Puritanism and the strength of their revolutionary potential.

Yet for all his misconceptions, in a sense the archbishop had a better intuitive notion of the collective religious life of his Puritan adversaries than many later historians: he quite correctly perceived that he was dealing with something more substantial than a variety of clergymen who refused to carry out parts of the prescribed ceremonies and indulged themselves instead in overlong sermons of questionable content.[3] Laud and his allies were all too keenly aware as well of the Puritan laity and of their propensity for unauthorized, potentially seditious forms of fellowship. They made sure to include the subject of "conventicles" in their visitation articles, using that one term to cover every type of unauthorized gathering.[4] Thomas Ryves, a civilian of long experience, summed up the matter neatly for the High Commission in 1631: "As privat meetinges are hurtful to the commonwealth, so these conventicles are to the hurt and breach of the church by errors and schismes."[5] At the height of Laud's campaign against this species of Puritanism one of his pamphleteers, Christopher Dow, even chose to interpret popular participation in religious exercises as a fully-formed church within a church, where nonconformist ministers duplicitously accepted the patron's presentation and episcopal ordination "but yet think themselves not rightly called to the Function unless they have withall gotten the approbation of the people of God, and of the Godly ministers."[6]

Dow notwithstanding, extraparochial religious exercises were not so many identical secret churches but rather informal improvisations by zealous individuals who shared a common need for a communion of the saints unleavened by the presence of their more carnal neighbors. The Broadmead Baptist Church at Bristol, for example, was originally neither Baptist nor a church of any kind but a gathering of "the awakened souls and honest minded people" in and around Bristol, who over a twenty year period met together regularly for fasting, prayer, and attendance on powerful preachers, including the widow of the group's original leader. In the late 1630s "when the clergy began to be high" they retaliated by boycotting the more obnoxious parish services, but until well into the 1640s they lacked the sacraments and were still willing to listen to ordained ministers when the sermon was acceptable.[7]

The Broadmead group were all laymen feeling their way towards new ecclesiastical forms at a hesitant pace. Clerical leadership, by contrast, might result in a faster rate of progress but also in a less thorough-going conclusion than a fully-formed Baptist Church. As early as 1629, under the sponsorship of Thomas Hooker, Chelmsford in Essex boasted "a company of Christians who held frequent communion together, used the censure of admonition, yea and of excommunication, with much Presence of Christ, only they had not officers, nor the Sacraments."[8] At about the same period there were similar organizations at Terling in Essex and at Stamford and Boston in Lincolnshire, where "the ministers and all the professours among the people have entered into such a covenant to yeeld professed subjection to the gospell of Christ, so farre as they conceive Christ requireth of them in their places in these tymes," while Laud claimed that convenanted groups could also be found in the west of England.[9]

To an outright Separatist, John Robinson of Leyden, these activities amounted to "spiritual vagabandry," a failure to follow up on the initial rejection of the parochial assemblies by gathering new churches where the sacraments could be properly administered in forms untainted by Antichristian corruptions.[10] Robinson failed to see that the "godly" laity might understand the meaning of Christian communion as the company they kept rather than as the specific ordinance of the Lord's supper, and that for them voluntary extraparochial exercises might provide an attractive and practical alternative to fully separated churches. When another thorough-going Separatist, Roger Williams, dismissed nonconformist conventicling as trivial, John Cotton, the leader of the Boston group, retorted with a kind of melancholy pride that "the meetings of the Separatists may be knowne to the officers in the Courts and wincked at, when the Conventicles of the puritans (as they call them) shall be hunted out with all dilligence and pursued with more violence than any law will justifie."[11]

There is an almost irresistible urge to see in Cotton's "Conventicles" the "nonseparating congregationalism" Perry Miller and Champlin Burrage pieced together into a doctrinal system from various treatises of polity. If the term is used in a strictly limited sense to mean the whole range of lay Puritan meetings which did not require repudiation of the Church of England as a prior condition of membership, then nonseparating congregationalism really was a viable mode of action chosen by substantial numbers of English Puritans before the Civil War.[12] When a distinct Independent position did emerge after 1640 its advocates naturally enough

4

cited the private fasts and prayer meetings of the recent past as respectable ancestry for their polity in order to refute charges of novelty or Brownist-inspired schism, but however convenient a polemical weapon, such identification of conventicling with Independent-style congregationalism is an anachronistic confusion, reading into the exigencies forced on an opposition movement the free choices available to their successors two decades later. Those who had patronized conventicles in the 1620s and 1630s did not necessarily feel obliged to defend congregational autonomy against nonprelatical forms of national church government during the disputes of the Civil War. John Bastwick is an obvious case in point, Colonel John Bellamy another and less well known one. Bellamy was a leading *jure humano* Presbyterian who played a central role in organizing the London *Remonstrance* against Separatism of 1646, yet he remained proud of his longstanding participation at "the private meetings of Christian people for prayer, Exhortation, Repitition of Sermons, or any other laudable and Christian familie, or neighbourly duties amongst the Saints," even though his Independent opponents gleefully brought up his past participation as proof of his current apostasy.[13] The Independent-Presbyterian split of the 1640s took on a peculiarly vicious tone in part just because it was a feud between former brethren who now found themselves in opposing camps, each regarding the other as the betrayer of the common faith.

Neither side in the controversy was really guilty of schism—or perhaps both were. What they had originally shared was not so much a common ecclesiology as a common form of response *faute de mieux* to the Puritan commitment to seek grace through the twin paths of the Word and the fellowship of the gracious during a period when both seemed in short supply. If the Word happened to be more effectively preached in one place than another, then parish of residence, arguably, should be no bar to those who would profit from hearing it elsewhere. According to the famous Puritan lecturer Arthur Hildersham, who excoriated Brownism and never lived to hear of Independents, "it were as intollerable bondage and tyranny to binde Gods people to rest upon the ministry of such as can not instruct them, as it were to compell infants to abide with such nurses as have neither sucke nor food to give them."[14] By the same logic, if a profitable preacher or another of God's people should also hold a private meeting to review a fruitful sermon ("repitition"), if such meetings should happen to serve for the edification of the godly by way of psalm singing, discussion of scriptural passages, and collective fasting and prayer, and if the participants should then wish to further their growth in grace by mutual watchfulness and admonition, perhaps formally certified by a covenant, then to restrain these exercises would equally be intolerable bondage and tyranny. Hildersham apparently thought as much, and so did a correspondent of Sir Robert Harley, who was himself a promoter of private fasts: among the "Queries sent to P[ar]liament 1640" in Harley's possession, one demanded "whether it be fitt that christians who meete together to fast and pray for subduing their sinness . . . not medling with any business of state, should be punished for it under pretence of conventicles."[15]

Although these meetings could be excused as a necessary and incidental corollary to the desire to hear a preaching ministry, for some Puritan laity they took on a centrality in their conversion experience which reduced even the sermon to the role of an external stimulus and the rest of public worship to outright irrelevance. Two redeemed New Englanders, for example, explained in their respective confessions that it was the advice, example, and fellowship of the saints in England which had enabled them at last to apply the preacher's words to themselves. One, a native of Sutton in Surrey, related that when he went to these meetings suffering from the classic problem of a hard heart, "they told me if I was obedient to the Lord it was enough And that I found [,] and so I was admitted to private societies of saints where I found much sweetness." The other, a better educated individual from Brampton, Suffolk, who eventually became a church deacon, attributed to his sojourn amongst godly societies the first fully effective wounding of his soul as well as his ultimate sense of assurance:

> And by a private meeting of private consciences I hard divers questions propounded and answered. And question being made when a man rested in duties, I was the man. And the grace I saw in christians did ashame me before the Lord, that christians soe young should manifest so much, I having had means so long. Hence I endeavored to get into private christian meetings at London and after, by other notes, I saw I was never one off the old stock.[16]

Both relations assign to public preaching a relatively secondary role, one good reason many members of the Puritan ministry considered private meetings something of a mixed blessing. Whatever the reverence shown to individual members of the clergy, self-selected societies of laymen who certified the godliness of their members posed a potential threat to clerical leadership and to the very idea of the church as a formal institution ordinarily necessary to the salvation and moral direction of residents of a Christian country. Arthur Hildersham, for example, was a case study in ambivalence. As at once a vicar of a parish and an understanding shepherd of the faithful remnant among his parishioners, he endorsed leaving one's parish minister in order to hear a more effective preacher, but then added the proviso that the faithful must avoid invidious comparisons.[17] At least three of his younger protégés in the ministry encouraged conventicles and he himself unequivocally declared that "Christians of sundry familyes may lawfully (even in these tymes and in such a church as ours is) in a private house join together in fasting and prayer," adding in no uncertain terms that "these tymes may also be justly called tymes of persecution" because "this truth and doctrine of god and this Christian duty of publick fasting (which god hath also streightly commanded to be taught and practiced when such occasion is given) is not only not allowed but opposed and persecuted."[18] Yet Hildersham also made sure to use his pulpit to denounce "any [who] through nicenesse, or idelnesse, or out of disdaine to joyne with the base multitude" preferred private worship to public, and from the same platform he singled out "many of them that have most knowledge, and are forwardest professours" for choosing what portions of the public service they would attend, heedless of the necessity to be present at all parts of the prescribed service.[19]

Hildersham was attempting to thread his way through a predicament common to the whole of the ordained Puritan ministry. Mindful of diocesan supervision, they had somehow to reconcile their public charge for the cure of souls with the very real possibility of a grass roots rebellion on the part of those parishioners who might otherwise form their most enthusiastic following. Hildersham knew at first hand the blandishments offered by the Separatists in the person of the mercurial John Smyth, and he had personally reclaimed from the latter's sway his fellow minister Richard Bernard, after which Bernard in his own parish of Worksop "did separate from the rest an hundred voluntary professors into covenant with the Lord, sealed up with the Lord's supper" in order, it was charged, "to keep your people from Mr. Smith."[20]

On the right hand, therefore, the Separatists, but on the left the multitude, whose indifference to their evangelical efforts led many Puritan minsters to find a positive value in the exclusionist aspirations of the godly. As early as 1586 the Elizabethan radical John Udall, no Separatist, still gladly accepted the accusation that his following, "the children of God," refused to mix with others and took communion only with each other. Udall replied blandly that "he hath allured disciples not to himself, but to christ; he would there were ten times as many."[21] Five decades later, John Cotton, who had gone part of the way towards organizing an exclusivist gathered congregation in Boston, Lincolnshire, quickly discovered in Boston, Massachusetts, that the rest of the road was easily traversed. "I durst not now partake in the sacraments with you, though the ceremonies were removed," he wrote back to England in 1633, soon after emigrating. "I know not how you can be excused from fellowship of their sins, if you continue in your place."[22] In the same year Thomas Weld, late vicar of Terling and another sometime conventicle keeper, saluted his former parishioners with a long contrast between their unfortunate estate and his own new-found happiness in Massachusetts:

> Here the greater part are the better part here Mordieci speaketh kindly to the hearts of his people Here are none of the men of Gibea the sonnes of Belial knocking at our doors disturbing our sweet peace or threatening violence, Here blessed be the Lord God for ever our eares are not beaten nor the air filled with the unclean conversation of the wicked, Here it is counted an honour by the worst to lay hold on the skirt of a Jew, Here if any be our Sanballets would thrust in themselves yet could not. Here the rudest have a charge and dare not breake it.[23]

Both Weld and Cotton wrote as embittered men. Until the arrangement had been disrupted by William Laud, they and others like them had come to terms with their pastoral dilemma well enough in England, accommodating the zealous members of their congregations without suffering substantial defections or abandoning their evangelical obligations. Created from a fruitful tension, the ministers' solution to the conflict between the needs of the many and the privileges of the chosen few was to live in two wholly separate ecclesiastical realms at once. Rather than forming a disguised "presbytery" within the established polity, as the Laudians imagined, the Welds and Cottons had chosen to remain full-fledged members of the national church and simultaneously to join the underground of popular Protestantism, where the minister might lead or follow or even suffer his clerical status to be ignored entirely.

At all times some Puritan ministers would not or could not ride this particular tiger. Sharing Hildersham's reservations without his qualified sympathy, they saw in extraparochial activities neither an opportunity for the exercise of their talents, nor a tolerable alternative to Separatism, nor even a necessary evil to be endured until changes in the national church eliminated the causes of lay disaffection. For some critics the predominance of laymen in private exercises immediately challenged the primacy of the clergy in church government. On a less theoretical level, the conventicles also represented unfair competition from individuals who could afford to be casual about both doctrinal orthodoxy and required ceremonial in a way foreclosed to the public ministry. Stephen Dennison, a London lecturer with a penchant for name calling, lamented in 1627 "the folly of many at these times, that had rather heare a man without a calling in some private conventicle, than a true Minister sent of God and authorized by the Church in lawfull assembly." He knew perfectly well, however, the audience his rivals would attract:

> Not Drunkards, Adulterers, Sabbath-breakers, Gamsters, Lyers, Swearers and such like, but rather such as seeme to be converted, which mourne for their sins and desire to know the right way to heaven, having bene in some measure wrought upon by the publike Ministery of the Church.[24]

Dennison's vulnerability may have arisen in part from his singularly pugnacious temperament, but a fellow London preacher of undisputed personal popularity, John Davenport of Coleman Street, revealed a similar siege mentality at almost the same time. Though he eventually became one of the patriarchs of New England, throughout the 1620s Davenport was the quintessential moderate, a charter member of the Feoffees for Impropriations who nevertheless protested his full conformity to successive Bishops of

9

London and who called for a common front "against those who oppose us in Fundamentalls." As a result, about 1624 he came under fire for ceremonialism from Alexander Leighton, then in the process of becoming one of London's best known conventicle keepers. Davenport replied in the name of all those whose overriding commitment to an established preaching ministry had allowed them to strike one compromise or another with uniformity, concisely summarizing what such men had to fear from their lay adversaries:

> . . . you have brought the matter to this issue, that I must answer, or else my ministry will suffer by my silence, whilest it is undoubtedly received by some, that eyther out of ignorance in these particulars, we take things as they are imposed without examining them, or, out of a corrupt mind, we dispence with ourselves in these things against our knowledge, for worldly expectacions. Make good either of these, and then, who will believe our reporte? who will regard our ministry?[25]

Dennison's controversy with his lay rivals ended up before the High Commission but Davenport's, rather more typically, did not. Whatever their degree of hostility or enthusiasm, most members of the Puritan ministry had learned how to live with "the children of God" by the mid-1620s, when the rise of William Laud brought about an alteration in the Church of England that ultimately claimed everyone involved as its victims. In a way Laud concurred in the misgivings of the moderates over the incipient anticlericalism of lay Puritanism, but he was notoriously careless in distinguishing among his Puritan opponents, and he had, in any case, perfectly understandable reasons for thinking that extraparochial activity posed peculiar problems for those whom God had set in authority over the church and state.

To begin with, the agenda of private meetings was not necessarily limited to the spiritual welfare of the participants. The Broadmead group from its inception "did cry day and night to the Lord to plucke downe the Lordly Prelates of the time, and the superstition thereof." When its members also entertained factious preachers visiting from Wales or New England-bound malcontents passing through Bristol (as they did in the 1630s), they served as an obvious medium for the spread of antiepiscopal sentiment.[26] Possibly, Bristol stood on the periphery of Laud's vision, but during his tenure as Bishop of London he certainly became aware of Thomas Hooker and his Chelmsford group, at least insofar as they included a ministerial contingent capable of transmitting Hooker's unpalatable teachings to the rest of Essex. "There be divers young ministers about us that seldom study," Laud's chancellor learned, "but spent thire time in private meetings and conferences with him or with such as are of his society and returne home in the end of the week and broch on the Sundaies what he hath brewed, and trade upon his stocke."[27] Hooker could be officially silenced, but a Henry Burton, who guarded his words in public, reserving his choicest remarks for private meetings, or an Alexander Leighton, who had no ministry to suspend, presented a far more serious problem. Both men definitely engaged in carrying their message to groups of the faithful outside of their home base of London, using their forums to "medle" in the affairs of state, and both eventually turned the connections acquired in the course of their conventicling to good use for the distribution of their antiepiscopal invectives. Neither man was easily stopped by the limited resources of the church courts and the High Commission: they would be stilled only in the Court of Star Chamber, where the charge would read sedition while the prosecution conducted a barely concealed trial for treason.

Laud's error did not lie in his initial recognition of the existence of the radicals but in assuming that they stood for the whole of the Puritan movement, and, equally, in believing every spontaneous or unauthorized religious assembly a dangerous amalgam of "Anabaptist" democracy, "Presbyterian" clericalism, and vestry Erastianism. Like others, Laud never could keep straight the difference between "Presbyterians" and "Anabaptists," but he knew well enough what he was afraid of, and the radicals obligingly seemed to confirm the stereotypes conjured up by both terms.[28] Misapplied though they were, even as terms of abuse both words had a consistent if overlapping meaning related to their literal denotation, and taken together they defined the context in which it became increasingly easy to consider every indoor private exercise a potential conspiracy and every outdoor meeting a riot in embryo. Regardless of his views on infant baptism, a man charged with "anabaptism" was being called an anarchist who allegedly founded political dominion on grace, excused the self-selected "saints" from obedience to carnal magistrates, and justified assassination in the name

11

of the gospel.[29] A "Presbyterian," whatever his actual opinions on polity, was supposed to come to the same bloody conclusions by more organized means. The Presbyterian caricature of contemporary polemics was a Protestant Jesuit, not a half-mad individualist like the Anabaptist but a disciplined conspirator bent on the establishment of an hierocratic empire where the Puritan clergy in conjunction with their vestry allies and gentry patrons would daily give law to princes:

> The doctrine and discipline of faithful *Geneva* are all substance: they are all gold. Oh if that Religion were here admitted, every presbyter shall be greater than a Monarch, and every Justice of peace above the Presbyter.[30]

Anabaptists were fanatics, and fanatics were presumably, if nothing else, honest about their intentions; Presbyterians were held to be more cunning. Scotland and Geneva were cited as examples of their ultimate goal once in power, but since the passing of the Marian exiles the English branch of the movement allegedly hid its real aims under professions of loyalty to the Crown. From time to time, however, it seemed to Laud and to those of his mind that zeal could get the better of policy and the pretense would apparently be thrown off—first by Leighton, then in quick succession by Prynne, Bastwick, and Burton. "Now Rome may cease all those bloody plots," Laud declared at Prynne's first trial in 1633.

> We have those amongst us who will hold up their doctrine against Kings and princes. . . . Yet all this is done in sanctified revelation. Nay, they go further; not only to censure and kill Kings and princes, but to allow rewards for them that shall do it.[31]

The archbishop must have been a nervous man by 1633 to think William Prynne a conspirator or *Histriomastix* a defence of tyrannicide. It was not, however, Prynne who initially confirmed for Laud the common equation between Puritanism, conspiracy, and murder. This honor went instead to Prynne's predecessor before the Star Chamber, Alexander Leighton. Leighton conspired with others to distribute illegal books and he undertook the keeping of conventicles; he would justify both, in print and before Laud, in the name of conscience, when conscience was held to be the byword of the Anabaptist and extralegal organization the sign of the Presbyterian. In particular, Leighton's publication of *Sions Plea against the Prelacy* in 1629 and his subsequent trial by the Star Chamber in 1630 had a crucial impact on the formation of Laud's concept of the Puritan opposition. Once formed, subsequent episodes involving first William Prynne and then John Bastwick and Henry Burton reinforced this notion until an inefficient "thorough" finally helped to precipitate the very crisis it was initiated to prevent. Just possibly, if Leighton and Bastwick had quietly practiced medicine, Prynne remained a capable barrister uninterested in theology and Burton confined his sermons to wholesome moralizing, then William Laud would have invented other incendiaries no less threatening, and his brand of "thorough" would have evolved anyway. The fact of the matter remains, however, that the monsters that alarmed Laud were the distorted images of real men.

II

The Protomartyr
Alexander Leighton

ALEXANDER LEIGHTON enjoys a somewhat anomalous reputation as the "fourth" member of the Triumvirate. Imprisoned from 1630, he had no direct part in the events of 1637 that cost Bastwick, Burton, and Prynne their ears, but he bore the scars of a similar mutilation, and contemporaries habitually lumped all four men together: *homo ejusdem farinae*," one professional letter writer had called Leighton. Of the four, he was adjudged the least subtle and, therefore, the most desperate. To the bishop of Ely he was a "Presbyterian Man of War"; to Archbishop Laud a man who went over the housetops of London with a naked sword in his hand. Leighton's most important book was said by Smectymnuus to be a work which "we durst not for feare of the *Prelates* keep in our studies."[1]

Leighton's was still a name to conjure with in 1640, but he was quickly forgotten in the rush of events of the next ten years. His output prior to his arrest in 1630 had not been large and, unlike Bastwick, Burton, and Prynne, he published nothing during the years of his imprisonment, nor did he resume his career as a controversialist upon his release.[2] Although he lived on until at least 1649 he was too ill to produce more than an autobiographical statement written no later than 1642 and published in 1646.[3] In recent historiography Leighton's works come up periodically, but the man himself remains just another pamphleteer, distinguished from the rest principally by a greater lack of caution. A few frequently cited rhetorical passages have obscured the significance of his career as a whole in illuminating the varied nature of pre-Civil War Puritanism. In the pursuit of his twin avocations of conventicler and polemicist Leighton exemplified the ways in which the Caroline underground functioned, just as his trial in 1630, in conjunction with similar cases a few years later, was central to shaping the Laudian reaction against all forms of Puritanism.

Both Leighton's career, however, and the various trials make sense only when their narrative context is reconstructed as fully as possible. Narrative is frequently the device of those who reject or ignore the concept of historical cause, and the form of narrative histories themselves can actually obscure the causal relationship between individual events. Even in the hands of a Gardiner, a rigorously chronological history can become a series of discrete instances illustrative of some general trend yet somehow independent of each other. But in the case of Leighton and the Triumvirate chronology really does matter: a slight shift in the sequence of key events, a few coincidences less, and both their lives and their historical significance might have been very different.

The beginning of the story is uncertain. Alexander Leighton was born in Scotland sometime during the last third of the sixteenth century, took an M. A. at the University of St. Andrews, entered the ministry, and at some point moved across the border into the north of England.[4] His name crops up as a lecturer in Newcastle in 1603, 1610, and again in 1612, but shortly thereafter he left the ministry or was forced out, for on 9 September 1617 he was entered on the roll of the University of Leyden as "Alexander Lichton, Anglus Londinensis, Ann. 40 Candidatus medicinae apud D. Brouwerum Anglum." He had come to Leyden to take the degree of M. D. and to join a fellow medical student, John Bastwick, at the home of Thomas Brewer.[5]

Brewer entered the printing business the same year, 1617, when he agreed to serve as publisher for the works turned out at the press of William Brewster, deacon of the English Separatist Church in Leyden. In their first year of business Brewer and Brewster brought out, among other works, new editions of the nonconformist classics, the Lincolnshire *Abridgement* and the 1570 *Admonition to Parliament*. The year following the press began to bring out tracts by opponents of episcopacy in Scotland, and with the publication of *Perth Assembly* in 1619 Dudley Carleton, the English ambassador, induced the Leyden authorities to suppress the operation. Brewer, however, escaped with relatively little trouble, while Brewster fled across the Atlantic to become a Pilgrim Father at New Plymouth.[6] In 1626 Brewer surfaced again, this time in Kent as "the general patron of the Kentish Brownist, who by his means daily and dangerously increase." He had reportedly also written a long manuscript "wherein he prophesies the destruction of England within three years, by two Kings: one from the North, another from the South." Brewer ended up in King's Bench Prison where he stayed for the next fourteen years, holding such conventicles as he could under the circumstances and composing a long commentary on the twelfth chapter of Romans. He died within a month of his release in 1640.[7]

No evidence survives to indicate what Bastwick and Leighton made of Brewer's prophetic tendencies or what, if anything, they learned from their host. He probably provided both men with their first introduction to clandestine printing, and both would subsequently make full use of their Dutch connections to bring out books too dangerous to be handled by English presses. Bastwick's opinion of Leighton, on the other hand, is on record: after Leighton's censure for *Sions Plea* in 1630 Bastwick "mayntayned both the contents of the said Laytons booke and the honestie of the man, and lamented his punishment wishing he had been there to have kissed his wounds."[8]

Neither man stayed at Leyden long. Batwick moved on to Franeker about 1619 and then to Geneva and Padua to finish his medical and theological studies. By 1623 he was back in England, settled at Colchester in Essex, where he remained until prosecuted before the High Commission in 1634.[9] Leighton stayed at Leyden long enough to take his M. D. there but was back in London by 24 September 1619, when the College of Physicians attempted (without notable success) to inhibit his medical practice.[10] At some point after his return he also began his special mission, organizing informal religious meetings of "the very best subjects, namely such as gather themselves together, to humble their soules for the sinnes of the times, for the safetie of *Sion,* and the deliverance of the

16

commonweale." The High Commission would have another name for it. "Doctor," said Sir Henry Martin in 1630, "you are a great *conventicle-keeper* (as they say)." The doctor's reply at the time to this "old calumny" would be, in effect, that "conventicles" were assemblies of papists and not gatherings of honest Protestants.[11]

Of all forms of extraparochial assembly, the private meeting for fasting and prayer was probably the most pervasive. When England sinned through the actions of her bishops or the inaction of her parliament, the godly were obliged to lament these sins or stand indicted of endorsing them through passive acceptance. If all other methods of reformation had failed, the faithful both could and should look for assistance by humbling themselves to seek after the Lord with fasting and prayer. "This course," Leighton announced in 1624, "will break the heads of the Dragons of your sinns; this will offer violence to heaven, and as it were inforce God to answer: this will be like an earthquake to your enemies, it will sink them, it will swallow them up."[12]

Of and in itself collective fasting in England was not a Puritan monopoly: general public fasts were enjoined for the whole country by proclamation as occasions warranted. But the Puritans had made the fast, along with the strict observation of the Sabbath, their peculiar observance in what has been termed the "calendary conflict" within the English church, and their passion for the exercise had led to unauthorized fasts and to ceremonies whose partisan character was inescapable.[13] Leighton, perhaps punning, had hoped to swallow up the enemies of the godly through his private fasts in 1624. Two years later his associate, Hugh Peter, at a private fast held with deliberate impudence on a feast day, began his sermon with a prayer for the conversion of the queen and added that "for the King he prayed God would commune with his Hart in secret and reveale unto him those thinges which were necessary for the Government of his Kingdomes." In another fast sermon of about the same period Henry Burton became downright menacing when he took his text from Joshua in order to hold up David's execution of "the Achan faction" as exemplary policy.[14]

It was no wonder if Laud and his party came to suspect fasts, especially if they were improved with sermonizing, so that by the plague summer of 1636 this traditional observance in time of national affliction "was deemed as hatefull as conventicles, the fruite of the vestry elders their vestry doctryne and the disciplinarian faction."[15] From a common ordinance of all English Protestants fasting was transformed into the hallmark of the opposition to Laud: after their punishment in 1637 Bastwick, Burton, and Prynne "were remembered with teares" at various "Assemblies of private christians to seek God by prayer and fasting upon extraordinary occasions," and upon the calling of the Long Parliament Nehemiah Wallington, the Eastcheap turner, wrote in his commonplace book, "O remember, remember (and let it never be out of your mind) that the year 1640 was a praying year," when "so many of Gods children did meet together in divers places in fasting and prayer for the King's good success in parliament," despite the prelatical "bloodhounds" sent to stop them.[16]

Leighton was an expert at the conduct of such meetings, but only fragments of evidence survive to indicate the identity of "the best subjects" with whom he kept his fasts. An unnamed informer of 1630 described Leighton's "faction" as "the same with the Jacobites, halfe Separatists." This remark probably only referred to their practice of holding unauthorized religious exercises in the first place and not to some explicit adherence to the congregationalist doctrines of Henry Jacob, but Leighton's connections may have actually extended to the members of the church founded by Jacob: in 1630 they were meeting in Leighton's home precinct of Blackfriars and one of them had already become his printer.[17] More revealing, however, is a letter of 1628 or 1629 (when Leighton was back in Holland) written to the pastor of the English Reformed church at Leyden, Hugh Goodyear, who had once shared Brewer's hospitality with Bastwick and Leighton.[18] The author of the letter, Ralph Smith of London, wrote Goodyear that "I desire to hear from you by D. Leighton how you do." Smith requested Goodyear to "help the doctor in his business" as well as to "Salute Mr. Peters if you can fitly with Mr. Winge." Mr. Winge was John Wing, minister of the English church at Flushing and earlier a supporter of Henry Jacob at the founding of the latter's Independent church at Southwark; Mr. Peters, of course, is Hugh Peter, forced into the Netherlands about 1628 after a stormy term as a lecturer in London.[19] Ralph Smith himself was fit company for the men he greeted in his letter: he had instigated Leighton's attack on John Davenport, and when he had to leave London for New England in 1629 the Massachusetts Bay Company considered his opinions too dangerous to allow him to settle in their colony, obliging him to take up his ministry with the Leyden exiles at New Plymouth.[20]

With Ralph Smith as one of his associates and possible ties to the Jacob Church, Leighton was mingling with London's sectarian fringe. His fame at running private exercises, however, also brought him more respectable company. At Leicester in the 1620s extra-parochial assemblies had multiplied, first under the patronage of a disciple of Hildersham and then under his successor, John Angell, who continued to patronize private "exercises of religion as prayer, exposition of scripture, singing of psalmes, repetition of sermons, and the like." Angell, however, did employ the Book of Common Prayer and in 1629 or 1630 he invited Leighton to one of these Leicester meetings for a debate on the lawfulness of its use, with the local schoolmaster standing by to take notes. No winner was officially announced, though Leighton's partisans gave out that he clearly had the better of Angell, and the doctor himself scribbled his objections to the Book of Common Prayer into the copy belonging to the building where the meeting had been held.[21]

Along with his sectarian associates, the incipient congregationalism of his conventicling hardly seems to fit Leighton's reputation as an ardent "Presbyterian," but the label derives from little more than his general notoriety and, probably, his Scottish birth. Leighton laid down his opposition to episcopacy in categorical terms without ever coming to specifics about what he would put in its place, apart from occasional ambiguous references to "the Discipline." He did not choose to explain which discipline this might be nor did he ever touch on the concept of a national church, on the qualifications for membership in a particular reformed church, or on the relationship between particular reformed churches. His one positive statement on church polity was a variation on a familiar formula which could comprehend either a presbyterian or a congregational form of discipline:

> . . . they [the learned] tell us from the word, that the church in respect of her policie and outward government appointed her by Christ, is not a Monarchie like unto the Kingdomes and Dominions of temporall Princes . . . but in regard of the choice of governours, by common consent is a free commonaltie, and in respect of the governours so chosen and governing according to Gods appointment it is an Aristocracie as Athens, Venice or the like. . . .[22]

Leighton saw private exercises as the refuge of the saving remnant and not as the forerunner of some future form of church polity, and nothing in his conduct or writing up to 1630 provides much of a clue as to how he would have sided in the Presbyterian-Independent feuding of the 1640s if poor health had not limited his activities.

Judging from his paean to private fasts in 1624, Leighton was already absorbed in these meetings by that date, and judging from his brush with John Davenport at about the same time he had already achieved a degree of publicity for the way he conducted them. With the exception of one brief interlude his conventicles were as close as Leighton ever came in his mature years to exercising the ministerial function to which he had originally dedicated himself, and during his long wait for the day when a change in the Church of England would allow him to resume his clerical calling these exercises probably absorbed much of the commitment that had initially gone to his first vocation. He went so far as to add to his slender list of works a whole treatise (never published) in defense of private fasts, and in his most famous book, among all the crimes laid to the bishops' charge Leighton held them to be at their most malevolent in their persecution of this last resort of faithful Protestants.[23]

Despite his complaints, Leighton himself never seems to have suffered from any kind of interference while he stuck to conventicling and refrained from activities open to a genuinely sinister interpretation. In 1624, however, he took to print, when the press of the "Ancient" (Separatist) church in Amsterdam brought out two books, *A Friendly Triall of the Treatise of Faith of Mr. Ezekiel Culverwel* and *Speculum Belli Sacri, Or a Looking Glasse of the Holy War.* The next year, 1625, the same press published his third work, an anonymous little tract called *A Shorte Treatise Against Stage Players.*[24]

The choice of a press in the Netherlands was significant. By 1624 London printers and stationers of Puritan inclinations usually risked handling only moderate criticisms of the established order: moralizing tracts and assaults on popery and "Arminianism" for the most part, with perhaps a few veiled allusions to objectionable politicians or churchmen. By contrast, really inflammatory works were almost always printed abroad and then smuggled into the country. In the Netherlands especially a thriving printing industry turned out a regular supply of books in the English language, the majority of them perfectly innocuous devotional tracts, military histories, and cutrate bibles. Along with this semi-legitimate trade certain Dutch printers for reasons of commerce or conviction also produced short "libels" on English affairs, many of them verse satires, and, occasionally, more serious wholesale critiques of the liturgy and polity of the established English church.[25] The number of such works increased so dramatically in 1623 and 1624 that James I rejected a draft proclamation against popish books until it was revised to include a ban on "seditious Puritanicall Bookes and Pamphlets, scandalous to our person or state, such as have been lately vented by some Puritanicall spirits."[26]

James probably had little interest in distinguishing between the various polemicists, all of whom attacked the English failure to support the international Protestant cause in language so nearly identical it has proved difficult to tell one author from another ever since their works were first published. Quite apart from his own considerable personal talent for invective, therefore, Leighton may have struck a raw nerve simply by adding one more voice to the chorus of Thomas Scott, John Reynolds, and Thomas Gainsford, who all attributed England's incapacities in military affairs to Catholic conspirators in high places and traitorous courtiers in the pay of the Spanish ambassador. Nonetheless, even among libelers, Leighton, as ever, turned out to be something of a special case.

Where Scott, Reynolds, and Gainsborough were all to a certain extent literary persons by trade, Leighton first decided to become an author when he was well into middle age and had never previously published anything other than his thesis on hypochondriac melancholy. Already in 1624 he seems to have been experiencing the sense of crisis that would make *Sions Plea* such an extravagant piece five years later. In his *Friendly Triall* he overruled the attempts of Ezekiel Culverwell to satisfy his doubts privately and took that prominent Puritan divine to task in print for deviating from strict predestinarianism at a time when "the Smooth Arminian adversary, who hath too many favourites amongst us, would make both a shield and a sword of this against Gods truth."[27] *Speculum Belli Sacri* with equal urgency calls upon King James, Prince Charles, and the Parliament of 1624 to undertake a "holy war" in support of Frederick and Elizabeth of Bohemia.

Leighton stood apart from the other English patrons of the Dutch press in another important way, his willingness to resort to the Separatists of Amsterdam. His connections in the Netherlands were entirely with émigré Puritan extremists, and he chose as his printer one of their number, the extraordinary Sabine Staresmore, and not as Scott et al. had done a member of one of the many Dutch firms. Staresmore's life story resembles one of the less memorable comic subplots in some Jacobean or Caroline drama, but he did have a hand in the production of many of the best known pre-Civil War Puritan tracts, and like Leighton his career vividly illustrates the overlapping sets of personal acquaintanceships which provided the basic means of communication for the loose-knit but very real community of Anglo-Dutch militants.[28]

Sabine Staresmore was almost certainly the younger son of William Staresmore, rector of Frolesworth, Leicestershire, and member of a distinguished county family.[29] Sabine as the second son of a second son could have had some aspirations and few prospects, the classic pedigree for the malcontent, and, appropriately enough, the surviving accounts of his career are found almost exclusively in polemics. He learned his Puritanism from a young nonconformist minister of somewhat radical leanings, but broke with him over the lawfulness of a written liturgy and became in 1616 a founding member of Henry Jacob's Southwark congregation. The "Jacobites" were not inaccurately termed "semiseparatists" because they insisted on the necessity of forming an extraparochial convenanted congregation complete with sacraments and yet they did not require a formal profession of separation from their members nor prohibit them from attending services in the parochial churches. This deliberate ambivalence coupled with a tolerant attitude towards internal disputes allowed the Southwark church to occupy a peculiarly strategic role as the transmitter of radical ideas within the body of English nonconformity: the organization appears repeatedly in the annals of the militant Puritans because it was virtually the only standing institution the Caroline underground possessed.[30]

From the first Staresmore seems to have considered himself a kind of missionary of the Jacobite left, dedicated to calling more moderate nonconformists out of their parishes into semiseparatism while he induced the genuine Separatists to come into communion with the Jacobites. He sought dismissal from Southwark to the Lee Separatist church in London, migrated from there to its sister, the Ancient Church of Amsterdam, then joined John Robinson's congregation at Leyden, and finally came back to the Amsterdam church about 1622, just before the death of its pastor.[31] Shortly afterwards a controversy broke out among the Amsterdam Separatists over the lawfulness of the Jacob Church and its form of covenant, and Staresmore with a few followers was predictably excommunicated. Staresmore then devoted himself to harrassing his erstwhile brethren until about 1630 when the new pastor John Canne, who was probably procured with his help, temporarily reunited the feuding factions.[32] Subsequently, Staresmore was to aggravate the quarrel between John Davenport and the minister of the English Reformed (nonseparating) church at Amsterdam, and then to disappear from Holland about 1635, surfacing again in England as a supporter of Roger Williams against John Cotton in their pamphlet war.[33] Staresmore played a minor part in the controversy over the City of London *Remonstrance* against the Separatists in 1646 and in the presentation of the Leveller's London petition of 1647, but his last major public appearance took place two years earlier, when by way of a grand exit he is recorded in 1644 in the company of just about every leading Independent divine then in London at a council called to advise the Jacob church on the problem of infant baptism.[34]

The exact manner of Staremore's introduction into the printing trade is conjectural, although he probably knew Leighton's landlord at Leyden, the publisher Thomas Brewer.[35] He was also a follower of Giles Thorpe, who served as ruling elder as well as printer for the Ancient Church, and upon Thorpe's death in 1623 he took over control of the Amsterdam press until at least 1634, when he was "the only English printer in the towne."[36] By virtue of his theology and eclectic associations Staresmore was able to broaden the scope of the press, so that in 1624 it brought out for the first time two books which explicitly rejected Separatism, Leighton's *Spelum Belli Sacri* and *Certain Observations of M. RANDAL BATE* (possibly also a contribution from Leighton).[37]

Leighton had been in the same place at the same time as Staresmore far too often for his choice of a printer in 1624 to be a mere accident. Both men had been at London, then at Leyden, then back in London again between 1616 and 1619. Moreover, Staresmore shared Leighton's enthusiasm for private fasts: in the summer of 1618 while he was in London negotiating with the Virginia Company on behalf of the Leyden congregation intending to emigrate to America, he had joined in a fast "with sundrie godly citizens" and ended up in the Wood Street Counter.[38] In going to Staresmore in 1624 Leighton was probably just renewing a friendship with a kindred spirit, but just such friendships and their periodic renewal were the means by which the more radical Puritans came together, whether their purpose was an exercise for mutual edification or the printing and distribution of a seditious tract.

Within a short time *Speculum Belli Sacri* had earned its author a certain kind of fame, and he found it necessary to absent himself from London while his house was searched by the officers of the Stationers Company, sent there he claimed at "the suggestion of the Gondomarian and Prelatical Faction." Peter Heylyn would later call the work "a booke composed of purpose as one noted to force church and state to a mutinous anarchy."[39] Its appearance caused Leighton quite enough difficulties for him to leave his name off his next piece, *A Short Treatise Against Stage Players*, when Staresmore brought it out in 1625.[40] By 7 July 1626, however, he had found it safe to return to London, for the College of Physicians on that date made still another attempt to inhibit his medical practice. They were no more successful than usual, and he continued in England another two years, now as something of a marked man. Laud and Sir Henry Martin had both seen *Speculum Belli Sacri*, and when Leighton was arrested in 1630 he would initially be identified as the author of this book until the contents of his last major work became known to provide him with still greater notoriety.[41]

Speculum Beli Sacri is a strange piece, without doubt the only handbook of military technique ever to begin with a favorable notice of Erasmus's *The Complaint of Peace*. Still, for Leighton reason and scripture alike sanctioned a defensive war in a just (Protestant) cause, and he offered his readers a "scantling of the Christian tackticks" extending to over two hundred pages of military minutiae punctuated by instances classical, modern, and biblical. The tastes of a reading public with an unsated appetite for military treatises probably accounted for Leighton's odd choice for his literary form.[42] In between discussions of encampment and strategy he tossed off shots against such familiar targets as Jesuits and crypto-papists at the English Court, and he distinguished himself by also going after the bishops and the established order in general. Common Prayer was "a *Key cold Leiturgie* galopt over, or cast through a sive with a many *parat-like Tautologies.*" Re-establishment of the Scottish episcopacy Leighton described as an angry God permitting "the stinking carkasse of the *interred whore, to be raked out of the grave, and the frogs of Aegipt to swarm in Goshen.*" Prince Charles was exhorted not to marry a Catholic in equally vivid terms: "be not unequally yoked; away with that Lincie-wolsie Match . . . it is a beastly, greasie, and a lowsie-wearing, unbefitting your Grace." As for the English bishops, "the very hearth that keeps in the fire of all this superstition," they were to resign their civil offices and cease to persecute "the stewards of Gods house" as a first step toward the abolition of the hierarchy. "Let Christ reign in his Ordinances, and let that maxime once be made good, in a good sense, *no ceremonies, no Bishops.*"[43] The same thesis in still more explicit terms would constitute the argument of *Sions Plea* in 1629, when Leighton next felt the urge to turn from fasting and prayer to more direct action against the enemies of the godly party.

An Appeal to the Parliament or Sions Plea Against the Prelacy had its genesis in the tensions accompanying the parliament of 1628-29. Leighton had begun *Sions Plea* in London during the prorogation of 1628, and then gone over into the Netherlands again, intending to finish the book in time to distribute a copy to each member of both houses when they reassembled.[44] His printer of first resort was once more Sabine Staresmore, though in his hurry he arranged for a second and improved edition to be brought out at the same time or soon after by J. F. Stam, a Dutch printer in Amsterdam whose firm had a long association with English language works.[45] Neither man worked fast enough, and though *Sions Plea* claimed on the title page to be printed "in the year and month wherein Rochelle was lost" (October 1628), this imprint was merely a deliberate misdating to remind readers of the precarious state of the Protestant cause. Leighton really finished his piece in January or February 1629 and was arranging its distribution from Utrecht in early March when parliament was dissolved.[46] The book was then distributed to the public at large, certainly with Leighton's knowledge and probably at his instigation.[47]

The tone of *Sions Plea* is more urgent than ever, at once fearful and hopeful, reflecting the apparent deterioration of Protestant fortunes in Europe during the preceding four years and the expectations of reform created by the assassination of Buckingham and the reconvening of parliament in the fall of 1628. Leighton maintained that moderate courses had proven ineffectual, but that victory was still within reach if the initiative was not lost and episcopacy was abolished before parliament ended its session. "But what need all these arguments, let this one plead for all: *aut hoc aut nihil:* either this, or nothing."[48]

If the most recent scholarly controversy over Puritanism may be gingerly sidestepped, Leighton's sense of urgency was less "millennial" than "apocalyptic"—he was preoccupied with Armageddon and neither supremely confident that he stood at the beginning of the thousand year reign nor in any obvious way unnerved by the resources of Antichrist.[49] He took as his text not Revelations but Amos 3:2, "you only have I known of all the families of the earth; therefore I will punish you for all your iniquities." As "the Lords owne people," the English nation, like Israel, was charged with a special responsibility for exemplary reformation. Sincere struggle for this end would accordingly meet with exemplary assistance, laxity or lukewarm moderation would provoke exemplary punishment. God, of course, could not lose the struggle with Antichrist but He most certainly would abandon the English if they hesitated in His cause because at that moment the conflict between Christian and Antichristian forces within England had reached a decisive stage where hesitancy amounted to surrender.[50]

With this rather simple eschatology as its initial premise the argument of *Sions Plea* makes sense within its own terms once the author identifies the ultimate enemy. As Rome is Antichrist, so the episcopal office originally ordained by Rome is Antichristian. It remained so in England even after the Reformation despite the Crown's assumption of the power to appoint bishops. Antichristian bishops, in turn, bore exclusive responsibility for all the corruptions still remaining in the Church of England. Paradoxically, because he was willing to recognize the maintenance of episcopacy as completely and irrevocably popish, Leighton could easily reject what he called the "quicksands of Separation" and uphold the essential purity of the English church: only take away this one anomalous episcopal element and the work of reformation would complete itself.[51]

To those who defended episcopacy by citing the example of the Martyr Bishops of the previous century Leighton had a similarly direct reply. A godly man might become a bishop but there were no godly bishops: corrupt at its root, the office would in time corrupt whoever held it. The original Protestant bishops of King Edward's day, newly come to reformation, understandably "did not see the evil of these things. Manie of them were painfull in labours, rich in works of mercie, and in the end some of these sealed their Repentance in their blood." Under Queen Elizabeth the bishops reverted to form, but the worst effects of their tyranny were mitigated by the queen, "some well effected Statesmen of the Nobilitie & others," who "were now and then *knocking* them over the shinnes." Now, however, far more wicked men filled episcopal sees, waiting on the time when they could resume openly the contact with the pope retained implicitly in their office, "so that whosoever were King (the Lord preserve our King) he should be but viceroy, as it were to our Jesuited Prelates."[52]

In the interim, in alliance with Hispanized courtiers the episcopal party monopolized all the positions of importance in church and state. Like new Diocletians they scattered God's people and made war against the twin essences of true religion, the preaching ministry, which gathers the faithful, and "discipline," which gives order and prosperity to the church. If it was too soon for outright popery, they could still spread its twin, Arminianism, "Spaines *newfound passage* for *Britain,* and the Low *Countries.*" From King John to King Charles, openly or undercover, the bishops had their hand in every major treason, including the Gunpowder Plot, which Leighton claimed was organized by Archbishop Bancroft in the hope of becoming pope.[53]

Mere civil prudence required the suppression of the prelacy but there were other, more immediate reasons for a chosen nation to eliminate this Antichristian faction. Since the cause of a cause is the cause of its effect, it followed that every reverse of fortune or nature could be laid to the bishops' charge as divine retribution for the "onely sinne of the Land *maintained by a Law.*" Even without direct treachery the bishops brought on the defeats at Cadiz and Rhé by the very existence of their office. English soldiers repaid an impatient deity with their blood for the passive tribute the whole nation rendered to Antichrist every time a suspended minister heeded an episcopal injunction to be silent or a parliament allowed itself to be dismissed without abolishing episcopacy. There was one and only one remedy left for parliament: "Strike neither at great nor small, but at these troublers of Israell. Smite that Hazael in the fifth ribbe: Yea if Father or Mother stand in the Way, away with them. . . . Make rather a *rotten tree* fall, then that the rotting droppes thereof should kill the sheep."⁵⁴

True to his premises, Leighton went after individual Hazaels by name. Laud and Bishop Richard Neile of Winchester were "Polydamnes twins, *Jannes* and *Jambres*," the Catholic Henrietta Maria "the daughter of Heth," and the recently murdered Buckingham a fallen Goliath. Buckingham's assassination called forth the most apocalyptic passages in the tract: the Duke's unexpected demise was a sign that the moment had come, and John Felton was an instrument of God, as impersonal as a lightning bolt, striking down the man who "sould the *fee*-simple of England to Rome that he might have the rent right." Parliament must follow the Lord, "who by giving of the first blow hath in mercie removed the greatest *nayl*, in all their tent and will not you follow home?"⁵⁵ The Holy War was now to be fought on English soil.

III

DAY OF JUDGEMENT

Leighton's Case

EVEN A MAN of Leighton's temper would never have been so bold nor would he have seemed so frightening except in the climactic years of 1628-29, when to all sides in England everything and anything seemed possible. With Leighton's trial in 1630 the opportunity had finally arrived for equating predestinarian Protestantism with Presbyterianism and parliamentary Puritanism with revolution by the simple device of invoking his name and all that it had come to suggest. Thus, Samuel Brooke, the master of Trinity College, Cambridge, announced to Laud:

> I dare say that their doctrine of Predestination is the roote of Puritanisme and Puritanisme the roote of all rebellions and disobedient intractableness in Parliaments etc. and all schisme and sauciness in the Countrey, nay in the church, itself. This hath made so many thousands of our people and so great a part of the gentlemen of the Land Laytons in their hearts. Besides where nothing is done the woods will overgrow the corne, as they doe.[1]

To be sure, Brooke was a posturing academic who thought he could secure the state with a theological treatise against High Calvinism; yet in 1630 even his fulminations were beginning to seem reasonable, thanks to *Sions Plea* and also to the behavior of its author.

Leighton had not actually set foot in England for almost a year after the publication of *Sions Plea*. Zealous man though he was, he was never particularly foolhardy, and while his tract circulated anonymously he himself remained in Holland as the new pastor of the English church at Utrecht. Typically, however, he lost this position by refusing to preach on holy days and returned to London, apparently hoping he would be protected by influential friends or perhaps just by neglect after the lapse of a year since his book's publication. It was a forlorn hope: he reestablished his household at Blackfriars in early January of 1630, was arrested on 17 February, and sentenced by the Star Chamber on 30 June.[2]

Trial by Star Chamber rather than High Commission indicated the gravity of the crime. Leighton stood formally accused of sedition and, implicitly, of higher crimes still. "The two Lord Chief Justices being present, delivered their opinions that they would without any scruple have proceeded against the Defendant as for Treason committed by him, if it had come before them."[3] Attorney General Sir Robert Heath hardly knew where to start extracting passages from *Sions Plea* for his speech at the trial, and his first draft omitted Leighton's most persuasive quotations. Heath soldiered on, however, finally producing an information and then a speech documenting the means, as he saw them, by which an obvious fanatic had brazenly advocated the massacre of the episcopacy and by implication the overthrow of the monarchy.[4]

The attorney general had not read the book very carefully nor the latter part of it at all, so it is little wonder he missed much of Leighton's meaning. Actually, for all his rhetoric, Leighton had not advocated killing anyone, nor did he indulge in the kind of suggestive language employed by a Henry Burton to give the impression he meant more than he wrote. Leighton was nothing if not direct and he very directly told parliament that they were to blame for Buckingham's death: if they had stood to their duty manfully and removed the duke from office before either his misdeeds or his power had grown to such a height, God would have had no need of a John Felton. As for the bishops, Leighton quite accurately pointed out in his answer to the information that he objected essentially to their office, and had called on parliament to abolish it, not to behead the officeholders. He certainly had libeled authority in a way that would be punishable in an English court of law in 1630, but nothing in the literal meaning of *Sions Plea* indicated that its author supported assassination and only one passage (which Heath managed to overlook) implied that he might condone revolution.[5]

Yet the Star Chamber became convinced of the contrary, and this conviction would remain with its members for the next decade. As the first major Puritan propagandist to be tried before Star Chamber and to undergo the full rigors of its pains and punishments, Alexander Leighton set a vivid precedent for those who came after him. He would always seem the one member of his sect fanatical enough to say outright what the rest really thought. "Then for the Puritan generally," Laud heard from an informant,

> they bee of his opinion, that the maine end of his booke, at which the Doctor shoottes is truth and that without any doubt; only he might have been more *moderate* and *discreet:* he hath failed in the *manner:* he wanted the *wisdome* of the serpent.[6]

Puritanism seemed to show its true face in Leighton, who, in his judges's eyes, would overthrow the established order by any means available, preferring the most violent. This notion hardly did justice to the nonconformist spectrum or even to Leighton, but it was peculiarly plausible under the circumstances of 1630. Given the existing biases of Leighton's judges, there never was a book nor a man better calculated to confirm their worst fears.

To begin with, the form of the book was extraordinary. Attorney General Heath admitted he had never seen anything of the like before. He was used to the short libel in print or manuscript which retailed a conference between the Devil and the duke or claimed Prince Henry had been poisoned by Sir Thomas Overbury and Overbury murdered by the earl of Somerset to keep him from talking.[7] *Sions Plea* was something else again, a whole book which managed to unite the diction and sustained invective of the libels with the seriousness, length, and multilingual marginal annotations of a theological treatise. As in the case of Prynne's *Histriomastix* three years later, the ponderous size of the book only seemed to make it more dangerous. "Libells of all kinds are in their nature wicked and odious, condemned in all ages: but for the most part, they are but short and smart, and therefore a Libell is in latine termed Libellus famosus, in the diminutive: this, is not Libellus but Liber defamatorious, a whole volume consystinge of 344 pages besides the Epistle and the preamble and there is the same phrase the same form throughout full of bitterness."[8]

This unremitting quality added to the power of the prose but it clouded its true sense, especially when so much of the argument ran by way of metaphor. Leighton was a medical man and in *Sions Plea* he was forever performing surgical operations of one sort or another on the body politic, cutting out episcopal tumors or lancing prelatical ulcers. Added to bloody Old Testament allusions, the anatomical diction could easily distract men already made wary by the stabbing of Buckingham in August 1628. And, read maliciously or just carelessly, Leighton did seem to approve Felton's act and encourage others to imitate it.

John Felton in his turn had added to the confusion. He claimed to have been animated by the Remonstrance of the parliament of 1628 and he died like someone out of Foxe's *Book of Martyrs*.[9] The temptation to identify him with the Puritans, especially parliamentary Puritans, was considerable. Playing on the "Anabaptist" stereotype as early as October 1628, Matthew Wren (not yet a bishop but episcopally bound) preached a "bitter sermon" before Charles I "against such as he styled Puritans, saying they were a most pernicious sect and dangerous to Monarcks, as bad as Jesuites in their opinions, that they hold the same Tenet that their Head Felton doth viz. that it is lawful to kill any man, that is opposite to their partie, and that all their whole doctrine and practise tendeth to anarchie."[10] When Leighton appeared on the scene calling upon parliament to follow Felton, the Anabaptist and Presbyterian caricatures merged. "This Presbyterian man of warre," wrote Francis White, Bishop of Ely, "congratulates a certain notorious murther, committed by a zelote of his owne devotion."[11] Felton's act showed the true meaning of Leighton's book and Leighton's book said openly what every Puritan secretly thought.

Wren and White wrote in the kind of polemical context conducive to deliberate exaggeration and even conscious misstatement. The intemperate language a man utters at the top of his voice does not necessarily describe the settled policy of his whole life. Yet Wren, White, Heylyn, and even Laud could not repeatedly argue that their opponents allowed predestinarianism to lead to political murder and not come in time to feel their lives in danger, at least Laud could not unless his complaints in his private letters to Thomas Wentworth in Ireland are also to be casually dismissed as propaganda by a man who really believed otherwise. In 1637 he wrote, "if some speedy order be not taken, and a round one too, I shall have too much cause to think mye life is aimed at."[12] Laud was speaking of the aspersions cast upon him by Bastwick, Burton, and Prynne but they were not the first to alarm him. In 1629 the same parliament that had incited Felton against his patron Buckingham had also threatened Laud himself. At the dissolution he confided in his diary that the parliament "laboured my ruin; but God be ever blessed for it, found nothing against me." Nineteen days later he received his first threatening letter.[13] Then within the same year came *Sions Plea*, a book Laud suspected to be the work of more than one man, and, as if to give point to its murderous theorems, three days after Leighton's arrest Laud received another anonymous letter threatening his life. Allegedly writing from the Temple, the nameless author ordered Laud to release Leighton or "you shall not see the end of your Expectation. I will say this I will effeckt my harts desire, and then, if I perish I perish. in the meane[while] pray god convert you or prepare mee for what shall befall me . . . god willinge I will see you eare longe."[14]

Leighton himself did his best to insure that any less than sinister interpretation of his intent was belied by his actions from the moment of his arrest: he refused to acknowledge the Antichristian authority of the two pursuivants who took him into custody and had to be carried from a public street on the shoulders of six men. Brought before the High Commission twice, he denied their authority too.[15] Before the Star Chamber, instead of displaying the customary contrition and repentance, he cheerfully defended everything in the book and answered the information by referring the court back to the marginal citations for proof of disputed propositions.[16] "A faire and full confession, and the worst of all confession," said Heath. "A justification of soe foule a cryme."[17] Finally, sentenced to an enormous fine, mutilation, and perpetual imprisonment, Leighton refused to accept his martyrdom without first effecting a melodramatic escape from the Fleet on 9 November 1630.[18] Recaptured and punished, he anticipated Bastwick, Burton, and Prynne by openly glorying in his wounds as so many signs of his Christian profession:

33

His wife went before him to the execution, and sayd As Christ was crucified betweene 2 theeves, so was hir husband led between 2 knaves. when he putt his neck into the pillory he sayd this is Christes yoke and that the spirit of glory rested upon him. when his eare was taken off he sayd Blessed be God, Iff I had 100 I would loose them all in the cause. He sayd his woundes were Christes wounds and such like passages.[19]

The man seemed reckless enough to have been involved in almost anything, and more unnerving still, he evidently had a band of confederates of the same stamp. At least some of the members of the Star Chamber knew of Leighton's conventicles, but they did not know the names of any of his associates, either in publishing or in holding prayer meetings. Leighton himself refused to reveal their identity except to intimate that he stood for legions. He told Heath he wrote *Sions Plea* at the behest of many "well-affected people," implied some of them were members of parliament, and then flatly refused to answer the article in the Star Chamber interrogatory demanding the names of his confederates.[20] Such a refusal had some precedent, but in Leighton's circumstances it justified Heath in calling for "corporal punishment, as in Pickering's Case, in a round manner, not to be redeemed but by confession of the names of his complices."[21]

Were it not for these unknown "complices" Leighton could have been shrugged off as a crackbrained fanatic and his followers dismissed in time-honored fashion as, in all probability, a gang of simple old widows with a sprinkling of poor apprentices not yet past their adolescence. In 1630, however, hard on the heels of Buckingham's death and the close of the most disorderly parliament in English history, the man loomed up larger than life: a terrible suspicion remained that he had influence with the many-headed monster and with its representative and incarnation, the Commons in parliament assembled. *Sions Plea* is *An Appeal to the Parliament,* a fact given full weight in the Star Chamber information, where Leighton and unnamed associates are charged with seeking to destroy the bishops, to "dishonor" the royal government, and "to stir up as much as in them lyeth your high court of Parliament then assembled to be the instrument thereof."[22] Leighton had magnified the power of parliament in his book, confidently maintaining that the "right noble Senatours" shared his thinking on bishops. After the three resolutions of the tumultuous last day of the Commons's sitting, it was all too obvious who the natural allies if not the abettors of such a man must be and what it was they truly aimed at. They would, "if they durst," Heath told Star Chamber, "reject the government of a King and intertyn a popular government."[23]

After Leighton's capture Laud had fretted over his confiscated correspondence in an attempt to identify his mysterious backers and eventually he came up with a "Mr. Pett of the Parliament house," presumably Maxmillian Petty, MP for Westbury, Wiltshire.[24] Leighton may actually have had a friend or two in the parliament of 1628-29, that particular parliamentary session may have been uncontrollable, it may even have been plausible (if incorrect) to assume that Leighton "invited the Parliament and people to kill the Bishops and to smite them under the 5th rib."[25] Nevertheless, it did not have to be assumed that parliament and people, however, roiled, would be inclined to respond to Leighton's invitation.

But this second assumption was made, and it points up a crucial misconception under which the Star Chamber by degrees was redefining seditious libel as unconsummated treason, thereby justifying emergency measures which would turn critics into enemies and eventually, in the trial of the Triumvirate in 1637, bring the whole of its procedures into disrepute. As of 1630 it was easy enough for prosecutors and judges, let alone those members of the Star Chamber also active privy councilors, to have a singularly clear notion of the fragility of public order. In that year they were routinely called on to deal with food riots in East Anglia and anti-enclosure risings in the West Country, and their recent memory would include instances of a pervasive hostility to government on the order of the mobbing of Dr. John Lambe as Buckingham's agent and the cheering crowd at the execution of the duke's own assassin.[26] From such a perspective the English people easily enough might seem an essentially passive but still volatile mass, prone to shortlived fits of mindless violence when provoked by interested or malignant agitators.[27]

Prominent in the latter category were religious eccentrics, Catholic and Protestant, who comprised a fair percentage of all of the defendants in sedition and treason trials from the reign of Elizabeth onwards. While few would dispute the disloyalty of the papists, or at least that portion of them presumed to be under Jesuit influence, the people were also held to include a large contingent of emotional, unthinking Protestants easily tricked into turning on church and state by groundless charges of popery and arminianism and by anti-Spanish jingoism. Heath invoked the shared consensus on the people's natural disposition in so many words in 1634, at Prynne's first trial:

> . . . what is more than to sett people against theyr soveraigne. God knowes how apte they are to suck in such Errors. I perceive that in this kinde theare is Little difference betwixt the Jesuitt and schismaticatt. Though theyre heads ar severed, yet they are Like Sampsons Foxes tyed by the tayles with Firebrandes to doe mischiefe.[28]

Since the people were not easily changed, the preservation of order depended on controlling the "firebrands" or "boutefeus" who deliberately set the spark to the dry tinder of popular prejudice. Again, in 1630 such men must have seemed too much in evidence: Leighton's was the fourth case of sedition to be brought before Star Chamber in less than two years, and he was also the last of a series of political defendants who seemed to make their intentions manifest by their contumacious behavior.[29] In every case the remedy was clear. Whether it was a mob or an obstreperous parliament, the magistrate must collar the ringleaders. Lacking direction, the rest of the crowd sooner or later with a little persuasion would revert to its fundamental passivity, while any remaining potential incendiaries would be terrified by the examples made of the most prominent of their sect.

This line of reasoning accounts in part for the extraordinary alarm which greeted Leighton. If he had not actually inflamed a crowd, a parliament, or even a lone assassin, this fact counted for less than the assumption that the people were easily inflamed. Leighton must, therefore, inevitably become their hero. "The common multitude" or "the Protestants at large (as some term tham)," Laud learned from his informant, despite their almost total ignorance of the contents of *Sions Plea* still revered Leighton,

> saying it was longe of the Bishops hee had that cruel censure, because hee writ a booke against them to the parliament, and

not one of 1000 dislikes him for it, for that report being generally received that most of the Bishops tooke part with the Kinge and Duke against the Commons.[30]

Leighton's successors would suffer from the same charge of "popularity" on the assumption that a man who appealed to the people against the bishops or the Court could hardly fail to find answering voices, more or less by definition. In 1634 Prynne would be sentenced in part for what the "common people" might think he had meant in *Histriomastix*. Archbishop Laud argued that the author of anything "that may have a treasonable exposicion" incited to treason whatever his literal meaning because "he that wryteth cannot tell of what disposicions his reder will be." Heath, by then a chief justice, rendered a similar verdict: he feared "the common people when they reade his booke, they will take him to bee a man of judgement and believe him," and consequently refuse to pay excises or subsidies to a government that allegedly squandered its revenues on court masques.[31] A polemic against the theater had been interpreted as an attack upon taxation and upon the whole of royal authority on the grounds that if the multitude read the book they could be depended upon to carry its author's logic to an antigovernment conclusion.

Heath's equation of the "common people" with subsidymen indicates the imprecision of his notion of that amorphous shape "the people." He was sure only that whether he was speaking of an urban proletariat or the forty shilling freeholders, the people were always, at least potentially, the enemy. They would always volunteer for the other army, the one that hated the existing government and possibly all government, because its generals alone were irresponsible enough to pander to popular passions. Writing in reply to Henry Burton in 1637, Peter Heylyn knew he was dealing with only the last in a long line of popular agitators stretching back to the first invention of presbyterianism: "I know it is a fine persuasion to make the common people think that they have more than private interest in the things of God, and in the government of the states: nothing more plausible nor welcome to some sort of men, such whom you either make or call *free subjects.*"[32]

The fear of violence was almost reflexive, and yet it was extremely limited, lacking any premonition of the Civil War to come. Once aroused, the people might be unanimous, at least within the geographical area affected, but they lacked the resolution for a long struggle. There might be murders, riots, regional risings, plots or coups, but neither Heylyn nor Heath at their most fearful could conceive of a sustained, nationwide conflict in which loyalties were sufficiently divided and sufficiently intense to keep the struggle going beyond the first major battle. Incredibly, the attorney general completely missed the most revolutionary—and prophetic—passage in the whole book, presumably because it did not fit in with what he considered the usual pathology of sedition. Leighton announced that "everie dessolution of a Parliament, without real reformation is against *right, reason,* and *record,*" and that the whole history of the English constitution, including precedents antedating the Conquest, allowed the parliament then sitting to remain in session no matter what orders "the common adversaries" procured from the king.[33] Somehow Heath overlooked these words and, revealing his traditionalism, singled out as the most clearly treasonable statement in *Sions Plea* an injunction to parliament to rescue the king from his evil counselors ("Athaliah's *Arminianised* and *Jesuited* crew") even if he did not particularly wish for liberation.[34] Leighton gave as examples of monarchs in need of deliverance Henry III, Henry VI, and Edward VI, but Heath probably had in mind a more contemporary instance, Queen Elizabeth and the abortive insurrection of the earl of Essex, which would explain his mistaken citation of Pickering's Case. Lewis Pickering had suffered corporal punishment because he had refused to name the author of a scurrilous verse he had pinned on Archbishop Whitgift's hearse in 1604. Leighton, however, was the author of the libel in question in 1630, and as such the most culpable of the criminals in a simple case of criminal defamation.[35] There was no need to threaten him with corporal punishment if he did not reveal his associates unless they were taken to be more important than he was, that is, unless they were not simply the spreaders of seditious rumors but the plotters in some intended insurrection capable of attracting ultraparliamentarians and rigid Protestants by virtue of casting the episcopacy in the role of the wicked councilors.

Heath and Laud were dealing with a man whose only real danger lay in what he convinced them he stood for. After his punishment Leighton spent the next ten years in the Fleet prison, his career finished but not his influence. Prynne, Bastwick, and Burton each in turn were implicated in supposedly criminal activities in part because of their presumed relationship with Leighton, who became, in effect, the official standard by which sedition could be judged. The earl of Dorset explicitly compared Prynne to Leighton in 1633, and in 1637 Laud indicated his total disgust with Henry Burton's *For God, and the King* by a simple equation:

> I am most shamefully abused by it. And I think there was never so impudent a book printed. Surely it is thought equal to Laygton's, and as desperate against the hierarchy.[36]

As the earliest to suffer Leighton created the mold of "boutefeu" into which his successors fitted—or were thrust.

IV

CIRCUMSTANTIAL EVIDENCE

Prynne's Case

THE FIRST TO JOIN Leighton in prison was the least likely candidate, William Prynne, for the least likely book, *Histriomastix*. Prior to his publication of this enormous attack on stage plays in 1632, Prynne had acquired considerable notoriety for his polemical tracts against "Arminianism," a term he used to cover the theology of Richard Montague and John Cosin and also any tendency in the Church of England towards ritualism or sacerdotalism in general. He had never gone after episcopacy *per se*, however, nor written any work requiring a Dutch printer. More often than not his books had a license and his troubles over them in the High Commission after 1627 had caused him only comparatively minor inconvenience.[1] Nor could *Histriomastix* be considered in the genre of seditious libels. Counsel for the defense quite carefully pointed out the difference: "Itt was not printed beyonde the seas, nor in corners, nor unlycensed, nor privately dispeirced." The license was obtained under somewhat dubious circumstances, to be sure, though this fact hardly sets off *Histriomastix* from Prynne's earlier writings or from the simultaneous efforts of Henry Burton.[2]

Equally, no evidence exists to indicate that Prynne organized or attended unauthorized religious assemblies. In the course of his career Prynne accumulated a remarkable number and variety of enemies, but whatever else they called him none of them ever alleged that he was a keeper of conventicles. Where Thomas Brewer in King's Bench prison, Leighton in the Fleet, and Bastwick in the Gatehouse all continued to preside over gatherings of their admirers after their imprisonment, there was apparently nothing for Prynne to continue once he was committed to the Tower, and no stream of former followers flocked to visit him there. The man was too much the individualist ever to be involved in a conspiracy.[3]

All the same, Prynne stood before Star Chamber in 1633 and 1634 accused of using his antipathy to the theater as a pretext to "infuse an opinion into the people, that for actinge or beinge spectatours of playes or maskes it is just and lawfull to laye violent hands upon Kinges and princes."[4] However surprised he may have been to be there, Prynne, in contrast to Leighton, did what was expected of a Star Chamber defendant. He apologized profusely for his careless language, expressed his loyalty in unqualified terms, and upon his conviction he sent up obsequious petitions to the king and the privy council confessing his fault and craving pardon; he did not get around to threatening Laud with the punishment reserved to those who shed innocent blood until the customary means of procuring remission of sentence had unaccountably but disastrously failed.[5] Since Laud had assigned his chaplain Peter Heylyn to draw up the basis for the indictment, Prynne not unreasonably concluded that the Archbishop was bent on destroying him out of personal vindictiveness because of his effective defense of traditional English Protestantism against popish intrusions in ceremony and doctrine. Prynne forgot, or chose to forget, that he was following Alexander Leighton, accused of much the same insurrectionary crimes, and that Laud was liable to see both men in the same light. After Leighton, whatever lingering doubts Laud may have had about the true intentions of the Brownists and their Puritan allies were dispelled by what he took to be the advocacy of tyrannicide in *Histriomastix*.[6] With Prynne's prosecution he had reached that stage of looking for hidden meanings where suspicions raised by Leighton might be verified but never disproved.

In varying degrees the rest of the Star Chamber shared Laud's state of mind. To most of them the superficial parallels between Leighton and Prynne seemed more significant than the very real differences. In both cases an overzealous precisian with a history of unlawful publishing had brought out a lengthy book dedicated to parliament and full of specious learning in which he insulted the queen and indirectly incited the people to rebellion and murder. The two authors even made the same defense, that when they cited the assassination of a wicked man as an act of God they praised the Lord for his justice and not the assassin for his deed.[7] In a manner reminiscent of Heath's judgment of Leighton, Chancellor of the Exchequer Francis Cottington found the size and relatively respectable form of *Histriomastix* good reasons to consider the book *more* seditious than the ordinary libel:

> ... it is not like other Libels: other Libels have been by persons discontented, some poor Rogues, scattered up and down; but here's a Libel in *folio,* and in Print, and it justifieth it self by Authors with an high hand, *That is there,* and *that is there.*[8]

Heath himself apparently was struck with the analogy, for his complaints about the length of *Histriomastix* repeated his earlier description of the unusual size of Leighton's work almost *verbatim,* while Sir Henry Vane remarked in passing that Prynne's "scandalous and opprobrious language" was just "the ordinarye style of all wryters of his kinde." When the Earl of Dorset finally voiced the inevitable comparison he found "that it is confessed of all, that Doctor Leighton's offense, was less than Mr. *Prynn's.*"[9]

Along with his chaplain Heylyn, Laud had been laying for Prynne for several years but they would have been neither so ruthless nor so convincing if Prynne had not appeared a second Leighton, or rather the second of a presumed band of zealots who would scruple nothing if left unsecured by authority.[10] Prynne had but "followed the humours of manye whoe if they cann but wryte wil not rest tyll they publishe themselves fooles in printe," according to Heath, while William Juxon as a bishop was still more terse: "Had this scurilous, virrulent, and infamous libell founde vente, the next booke would have been meere treason." Dorset added his assent a bit more poetically: "Such swarms of Murmurers as this day disclose themselves, are they not fearful Symptoms of this sick and diseased time?"[11]

Laud scented a conspiracy behind the composition of so long a work as *Histriomastix,* as he had in the authorship of *Sions Plea,* and he may possibly have thought it the same conspiracy in both cases.[12] But there was no need for conjecture or analogy in order to satisfy Star Chamber about the ties between Prynne and Leighton. Prynne boldly cited Leighton's *Speculum Belli Sacri* "divers times" in his own work in a manner which seemed to reveal the true intentions of both authors, for Prynne coupled his references to Leighton with further citations to the *De rege et regis institutione* of the Jesuit Juan de Mariana, tutor of Cardinal Bellarmine and apologist for tyrannicide. Heylyn, who alone had the patience to check out Prynne's marginalia, advised Attorney General William Noy:

> it were worth the asking whie Mr. Pryn should so often Cite Laytons speculum belli sacri, and Marianas book de Regis institucione and whie hee should so magnifie both these bookes and Authores as he doth, may it not bee that he agreeth with them in their mutinous and pernitious expsicions And that hee takes as well the arguments as he doth the Authores.[13]

Noy followed Heylyn's notes closely, even his pedantic objection to an alleged mistranslation of a Latin passage by Bodine, and he duly incorporated the citations to Leighton and Mariana into the information against Prynne.[14] Prynne's counsel replied that his client "adhereth to their meaning so far and wherein they are agreeable to the Law," to which Cottington rejoined: "that which he doth apply of any Author is his own."[15]

In actuality Prynne had cited Leighton and Mariana a few times in an eight hundred page book composed mostly of citations and at no point did he allude to the former's hostility to episcopacy or the latter's justification of regicide.[16] His conviction, the severity of his sentence, and the ultimate execution of the whole of that sentence despite his public contrition seem foregone conclusions now only because of Star Chamber's subsequent reputation (earned in large part at Prynne's two trials) and because of the oddest feature of an odd case, the extraordinary unanimity of all the members of the court in holding William Prynne an immediate menace to the security of the realm. Laud, of course, needed no convincing on this point after his encounters with Prynne and Burton in the High Commission, but in purely ecclesiastical matters the rest of the Star Chamber did not necessarily follow his lead: the limits of Laud's strength in the court had, in fact, been fairly well indicated just one year earlier in the trial of Henry Sherfield, recorder of Salisbury, for an act of iconoclasm in his parish church. Sherfield was an old political enemy, and Laud had demanded a stiff sentence for a man who symbolized for him both lay inconformity and vestry usurpation of episcopal prerogative, but he had been opposed by fully half of the Star Chamber, including Dorset, Heath, Chief Justice Sir Thomas Richardson, and Secretary of State Sir John Coke, all of whom held out for mild or token punishment.[17] In Prynne's case, however, the crime seemed to threaten far more than the right government of the church as its current primate happened to conceive it, and every member of the Star Chamber concurred with Laud in his severe sentence except for those who held out for somewhat harsher penalties. As at Leighton's trial, the chief justices declared that although the charge read seditious libel the defendant could have been prosecuted for treason in a common law court. Heath announced that he grounded his sentence on those passages in the book "soe expresslye layde that for them it would have been no strayne of lawe to have him arrayned for highe treason," while Richardson came to exactly the same conclusion in a wordier manner and then for good measure agreed with Laud in his suspicion "that there were many heads and hands therein besides" Prynne's own.[18]

Richardson arrived at his verdict even though he implicitly rejected Laud's claim that the meaning of *Histriomastix* was to be determined solely by its likely effect on a violence-prone reader. The chief justice of the King's Bench held the author's original intention certified under his oath a good defense "where the word standeth equal, as that you may take the Intention this way, or that way, with the right-hand or left-hand," but irrelevant to a defendant whose "words are plain and clear" despite his never so much as mentioning the king and queen.[19] Counsel for the defense had quite correctly observed, as politely as possible, that the Star Chamber had made up its mind to put a treasonable interpretation on Prynne's words whatever he wrote. If he *had* mentioned Charles and Henrietta-Maria by name in order to exempt them from his historical strictures on play-going sovereigns he really would have been vulnerable to a charge of compassing their deaths while barely camouflaging his intention through a clearly specious exemption:

But you say, he Shoulde have saide I meane not the King nor Quenne, I except them. If he had donn so, I shoulde have rather thought it an Ironnicall Exprobation, then any Just exception.[20]

Execution of the sentence without any degree of remission rested on the same presumption that behind *Histriomastix* lay a long standing traitorous conspiracy, in Chief Justice Richardson's words, "to set up the *Puritan* or Separatist faction."[21] Prynne gave the Star Chamber what it had never been able to obtain from Leighton, a public confession and retraction of exemplary abjection, which should have merited some mitigation in his penalty. Even Leighton had received the unasked for remission of half of the mutilations to which he had been sentenced, but in Prynne's case they were carried out in full, an act of severity which served a purpose only if its intention was to terrify the rest of the participants in the assumed plot. Similarly, to carry out the sentence of perpetual imprisonment after Prynne's humiliation and recantation was not to punish a penitent libeller but to take out of circulation a man still considered dangerous when "this courte cannot doome him to suffer according to the quallitye of his offence" by eliminating him permanently.[22]

Curiously, of the four Puritan authors tried by the Star Chamber, William Prynne, even on the face of it, was the least obnoxious to authority. He lacked Leighton's uncompromising extremism, Bastwick's habitual recklessness, or Burton's penchant for innuendo, and as of 1633 he had no known sectarian associates. It would take some doing to turn him into a confederate of the likes of Leighton; indeed, it would take a Star Chamber prosecution and the loss of his ears. His moderation rebuffed, Prynne grew immoderate and wrote his threatening letter to Laud, thereby giving the archbishop reason to believe that moderation was just a pose affected by Puritan zealots to conceal deeper designs. "Our main *Crime*," Laud would say the next time he had occasion to try Prynne, "is (would they all speak out as some of them do) that we are Bishops."[23] Thanks to earlier preconceptions confirmed by Leighton and then reinforced by Prynne, Laud was doing his best to crush a phantom conspiracy by means which discredited episcopacy and turned his victims into real conspirators. In the Tower an exasperated Prynne grew more violent in his prose and more

45

wholesale in his attacks on the Laudian version of episcopacy, exhorting suspended ministers (in the manner of Leighton) to ignore inhibitions "and goe on courageously in their Ministery in despite of them."[24] He ceased looking for "godly Bishops" from the recent past to contrast with the excesses of the "lordly prelacy" under Laud and allowed himself language which could be taken to mean that the whole episcopal order as constituted in England was Antichristian in origin. A tract smuggled out of the Tower and published in the Netherlands in 1637 asserts that there have "been more notorious Traitors Rebells and conspirators, of Bishops then of all other ranks of men in the world" and goes on to ask rhetorically why if episcopacy is of purely human establishment and past experience has proven it both unnecessary and dangerous, it can not be dispensed with altogether "as they do in all reformed churches, who have quite cashiered them long agoe?"[25] Even *The Antipathie of English Lordly Prelacie*, which William Lamont sees as Prynne's first forthright commitment to ecclesiastical radicalism, was actually begun in the Tower, though not completed nor published until 1641.[26]

The works Prynne did complete and smuggle out of prison between 1634 and 1636 were too extreme for the London presses, and he turned out of necessity to the Netherlands for the first time, becoming involved at last with the Puritan fringe of Leighton and Bastwick, Staresmore and Canne, to which Laud had already consigned him. By 1636 he was willing to compare himself in print with Bastwick, Leighton, and ultimately Thomas Brewer as fellow victims of the prelates' murderous malice and their more than popish lust for *jure divino* power.[27] When Bastwick and Henry Burton actually joined Prynne in clandestine printing in 1636 the stage was set for the tragicomic joint trial and martyrdom of all three.

V

Day of Wrath

The Triumvirate and Their Trial

WHERE PRYNNE HAD DONE his best to keep out of prison in 1633, about the same time John Bastwick seemed positively bent on getting inside. A friend of both Prynne and Leighton, Bastwick distinctly resembled the latter in his activities.[1] During his eleven years at Colchester he too mixed physic and divinity in about equal proportions, so that he was eventually denounced to the High Commission. The records of Bastwick's trial include the charge that he spread his opinions by word of mouth as well as by his writings, but do not mention whether he used private exercises for his forum.[2] On the other hand, Bastwick's brother-in-law Thomas Cotton definitely did patronize such activities as well as maintain "some pevish intelligencer in London" in order to acquire antiepiscopal and antigovernment invectives, "which he usually reades in the street evry markett daye att Colchester about whom the zealants thronge as people use where Ballads are sunge." To Cotton's house in 1634 came none other than Henry Burton "and preached a seditious sermonn att his privat church which pleased him so well, as he caused him to preach the same sermon upon a Lecture days att Colchester."[3] The irrepressible Bastwick was hardly likely to be far behind either his brother-in-law or his old friend

47

Burton in frequenting and fostering conventicles in Colchester and vicinity.

In 1634 when the High Commission finally caught up with Bastwick he was charged with defaming the prelacy, denigrating the liturgy, and rejecting *jure divino* episcopacy, as well as with maintaining Leighton's innocence during the latter's trial. Bastwick subsequently gave out that he was fined and imprisoned at Laud's instigation because his attacks on Roman Catholic episcopacy in two books printed in Holland inadvertently hit too close to the mark among the popishly affected English bishops, but this story amounted to little more than self-dramatization. He was actually called before the High Commission on complaint of the minister of Colchester, and his two books were initially entered only as corroborative evidence after he attempted to discredit the testimony of several of the witnesses by accusing them of malice. In the final sentence, however, the doctrine, foreign publication, and allegedly secret distribution of the two tracts were also held against him.[4]

Trial by the High Commission was nowhere near as serious as trial by the Star Chamber. On several counts the former's procedures were the more arbitrary but the penalties it could inflict were more limited and it usually remitted most of an offender's sentence once he humbly acknowledged his transgression.[5] Bastwick, however, announced to the commissioners that "he was like Paul before Nero" and after taking the *ex officio* oath refused to answer a portion of the interrogatories. Convicted after a lengthy trial, he declined either to confess his fault or pay his fine and give surety for good behavior, and the commissioners ordered him imprisoned until he complied with their sentence.[6]

Now confined to the Gatehouse, Bastwick took advantage of the relaxed regime there to get his *Apologeticus ad Prasules Anglicanes* published in the Netherlands in 1636 and to entertain admirers of his zeal, who did him "smal favors" and loaned him money. This Gatehouse circle included a young apprentice named John Lilburne, already a hardline Separatist, and a number of others whom Bastwick subsequently described as "Independents." By means of these same individuals Bastwick's first English book, the *Letany*, was circulated in manuscript while Lilburne (according to Bastwick) saw to the business of its printing.[7] Lilburne later denied any direct connection with the printing of the *Letany* but he did go

48

over to the Netherlands, and somehow the *Letany* ended up with James Moxon, an English printer of Independent inclinations who then resided in Delft.[8] In November of 1637 William Bridge and Jeremiah Burroughs, both prominent nonconformist divines, again of Independent inclinations, were observed in "disguised habits" smuggling the books from Delft to Yarmouth where they were to be distributed by the local "barme Conventiclers." Moxon, the printer, subsequently moved on to Rotterdam, where he became a supporter of the Independent English church in that city. This congregation then called Burroughs to its ministry in 1638, closing the circle. Individual contacts were still the core of the Puritan exile community in the Netherlands.[9]

The *Letany*'s sustained antiepiscopal invective and its mock liturgical form as well as its numerous, rather earthy puns have earned Bastwick a reputation as something of a folk humorist, the one Puritan with a sense of fun, but his judges probably found the piece less than remarkable. The High Commission and the Star Chamber routinely handled similar cases of libels in verse or prose directed against both private and public persons, and the *Letany* derived its peculiar importance mainly from its author's association with Prynne and Henry Burton, although the printing and distribution of both of Bastwick's books were largely separate from the simultaneous operations undertaken for the other two men.[10] At his trial Bastwick was able to declare that except for Prynne and Burton he was not acquainted with anyone charged in the information with the circulation of seditious literature.[11] Rather, his associations remained as ever thoroughly sectarian and his lack of caution was still monumental: already a prisoner of the High Commission, he was busy issuing signed denunciations of the hierarchy. William Prynne in similar circumstances at least had the sense to remain anonymous.

The last member of the ill-assorted Triumvirate was a queerer fish still. Henry Burton had ruined his prospects as a courtier by opposing Laud and Neile and had then become a London lecturer hovering somewhere between the upright strict Calvinism of Prynne and the sectarian intrigues of Bastwick. Like Prynne, he had restricted his printed works to attacks on popery and on Montague and Cosin, never needing to go beyond issuing un-licensed or improperly licensed books from the London press. The names Burton and Prynne were regularly associated together between 1627 and 1630, but Burton had also preached at Thomas Cotton's conventicle in Colchester and as an old friend of Bastwick he took a keen interest in his case before the High Commission, visiting him in prison on two or three occasions.[12]

Burton was the leading practitioner of the art of saying just too much, infuriating his enemies by hints and parallels without giving them sufficient grounds for successful prosecution. In one instance in 1627 he procured a license for the text of one work and then before publishing it tacked on an offensive but ambiguous epistle full of veiled warnings to Buckingham.[13] *Israels Fast,* another effort employing similar tactics, had its origin in August of 1626 or 1627 at a general fast when he had preached a sermon out of the seventh chapter of Joshua calling for the removal of the English "Achans" by the English David and the elders of the English Israel in parliament assembled. Somewhat revised, the sermon was published in 1628 with a few of Burton's typically pointed allusions. One edition bears the provenance "Rochel" and the preface compares "the Achan faction" in England to "the *Guisian* faction in *France,* who were too hard for King *Henry* the Third."[14] Burton had probably brought the piece out before the duke of Buckingham had gone to join the duc de Guise and in the printed version he prudently left the Achans unnamed, although the parallels with Buckingham were evident throughout the text. When a special session of the High Commission demanded to know just whom he meant by the Achan faction, he blandly replied, "The Jesuiticall faction: and no more could they squeeze from me, so as not knowing what to do with me, they let me go."[15] Then Alexander Leighton gave the game away in *Sions Plea* by praising "An Able Pastor" who in preaching a sermon in London at a late general fast "under *Joshua* his removall of the excommunicate thing; tould us in plain tearmes, that the main thing was that damnable *Hierarchie,* who made no matter of the sinkinge of the Church, and State; so they might swimme in their *honours,* and *pleasures.*" Leighton's allusion to Burton was caught by White, Bishop of Ely, who had a long standing feud with Burton, and picked up from him in turn by Peter Heylyn. So it stood revealed at last: in *Sions Plea* one of the "Presbyterian backbiters" had carelessly let out what all the "furious Aërian heretics" including Burton aimed at, the massacre of the hierarchy.[16]

Burton himself thought the hour for forthright declaration to be at hand. He had escaped the fate of Leighton, Prynne, and Bastwick only to watch the continued growth of ritualism and *jure divino* episcopal claims throughout the 1630s. The waiting game just did not work, and it was time the moderate man with good connections gave way to the uncomprising witness for Christ. Burton preached against all the ceremonies and gave up using them himself while he selected the moment for the most dramatic possible act of self-sacrifice.[17] On Guy Fawkes Day, 1636, he preached two strident sermons in which he first declared that "the tymes are nowe soe that hee which will feare God must not feare to lay downe his Ministery" and then dramatically discovered for his auditory a second Gun-powder Plot in the form of the insidious infusion of ceremonial and Arminian innovations into the Church of England, all of which he catalogued in some detail. The plotters remained rather vaguely "those false friends which are about the Kinge who under pretense of freyndshipp doe goe about to undermine and overthrowe both church and state," but it was easy enough to spot them by their attempts (under the pretext of avoiding controversies) to silence those faithful ministers who plainly opposed "Armenian heresyes which do combine with popery":

> This is a cunning way indeed as Father Latimer said Perceave you nothinge. doe you not see that there are Plottes to make as great a change as ever those [Gunpowder] Traitors would have done, doe not our Eyes see those things practised and goe on stepp by stepp and that with a great prevaylinge hand-doe you not see how impudently bold, they are grown, when they dare bring in new lawes new Rites, new Ceremonyes into the Church of God aganst Lawes statutes & Acts of Parliament.[18]

The inevitable summons from the High Commission followed and was ignored while Burton shut himself up in his house to revise the sermons, along with an appeal to the nobility, for publication. "The while the Prelates Pursuivants, those Barking Beagles ceased not night nor day to watch, and rap, and ring at my doores, to have surprised me in that my castle, nor yet to search and hunt all the Printing houses about *London,* to have prevented the coming forth of my Book, which they heard to be at the Presses." Burton managed to have his works printed secretly, however, and on 1 February 1637 editions of *For God, and the King* and *An Apology of an Appeal* arrived in London calling for a new parliament to overthrow Laud and, by implication, the whole episcopal order: "both God and the King, that is, the justice of Gods Law, and mans law shall conspire together to root them out." On the same day their author was finally arrested.[19] Burton now took his place alongside Bastwick and Prynne in a Star Chamber information filed the following March.[20]

The information names all three men as jointly and severally responsible for Burton's two books, for Bastwick's *Apologeticus* and his *Letany* (still only in manuscript), and for two anonymous tracts which had appeared in 1636, *Newes from Ipswich* and *The Divine Tragedy*. Both tracts were widely attributed to Prynne and/or Burton, and neither man denied their composition at the trial as emphatically as Bastwick.[21] *Newes from Ipswich* is a classic short libel in coranto form about the activities of Matthew Wren, by then Bishop of Norwich, and differs from the rest of its genre only in the heavy use of marginal citations. Neither its author nor printer is definitely known, but the circumstances of its distribution point strongly in the direction of a Dutch press. *A Divine Tragedy*, a short collection of "authenic" tales of the punishment meted out to sabbath breakers, is almost certainly Burton's, though Prynne may have composed the last and most abusive section detailing his mistreatment by Attorney General Noy in 1633 and Noy's consequent horrible death. The book was definitely printed in Amsterdam at the press of J. F. Stam, the publisher of the second edition of *Sions Plea*. Stam also brought out Burton's *For God, and the King* and *An Apology of an Appeal* along with five works in 1636 and 1637 indisputably by Prynne.[22]

Staresmore's disappearance from Amsterdam about 1635 accounts for the diversion to Stam of business that would normally have gone to the Ancient Church.[23] John Canne, the Church's new minister, eventually took over the press, resuming publication in 1637 with Prynne's *A Quench Coale*. An advocate of rigid Separatism, Canne entirely replaced Stam within the year as the Amsterdam printer of Puritan books, and he may have started operations still earlier, in 1636, with second editions of *A Divine Tragedy* and Burton's two tracts as well as the only edition of Prynne's *A Looking Glass for all Lordly Prelates*.[24]

Prynne and Burton had now joined Bastwick and Leighton as patrons of the Dutch press because of the increasingly radical tone of their works and death, imprisonment, or disability of the London stationers on whom they had previously depended.[25] Unavoidable as this decision probably was, it still required Prynne to commence and Burton to deepen an involvement with the sort of Puritan zealots both men might have preferred to keep at arm's length if they had not needed the skills of the segment of English Puritanism most experienced in the business of smuggling books. Both men would inevitably be judged by the company they kept, and the company was choice.

In early February 1637 just when Burton's two tracts were arriving in London, "a great bundle of these kind of prohibited books" was seized at the home of one Rice Boye, "a silenced minister dwelling in an alley in Coleman Street."[26] Once again, casual personal connections provided the only organization the clandestine book trade possessed. Boye, an outright Separatist of eccentric theological opinions, had come into contact with Canne and possibly Staresmore in 1630 as a member of a fully Separatist splinter group of the Jacob Church and had printed an odd tract, *The Importunate Beggar,* with Stam in 1635.[27] Boye's earlier career as a preacher in the West Country qualified him equally well to act as the contact with the great Somerset clothier John Ashe, who was arrested for distributing *Newes from Ipswich* at the same time that Boye's house was searched.[28] Later, in 1638, another Separatist inhabitant of Coleman Street served as a "privat foot post" for carrying messages and pamphlets between London and Leyden, where Willem Christiaans, a sympathetic Dutch printer, turned out prohibited English books, including Bastwick's *Answer* to the Star Chamber indictment and a Dutch version of *Newes from Ipswich* designed to "make the Bishoppes crultie knowne to all Nationes."[29] Each of these relationships was informal in origin and intermittent in duration; collectively, they could appear a dangerous combination of nonconformists and sectaries, confirming the often repeated charge that nonconformists were simply Brownists without the courage of their convictions.

The time for "thorow" was at hand. In an attempt to quiet giddy spirits for all time the trial of Bastwick, Burton, and Prynne deliberately received wide publicity. Ordinarily, seditious books did not merit the dignity of an official reply and public accounts of the prosecution of their authors were limited to rumor, but for this occasion Christopher Dow and Peter Heylyn received commissions to reply to Burton with a few side shots at Prynne. Laud also broke a precedent by publishing his speech at their censure and eagerly distributing copies of his tract to anyone evincing even a mild interest in the subject.[30] The proceedings themselves were less judicial than ritualistic. Star Chamber had its men, it thought it knew from bitter experience what they were up to, and felt no need for judicial niceties nor even for further investigation to make a more accurate assessment of the nature of the enemy. Laud particularly knew enough for his own satisfaction without more detailed inquiry except perhaps for evidence to verify his moral certainty that his old enemy John Williams was part of the conspiracy.[31]

Viewed either as an exemplary trial or just as a piece of detective work, the Star Chamber proceedings against the Triumvirate were a disaster.[32] Laud spent his time fruitlessly scanning Burton's sermons and *Newes from Ipswich* for internal evidence of Prynne's authorship when the Star Chamber information could simply have included the four works Prynne definitely did compose in 1636.[33] These omitted works contain passages quite as violent as any from the tracts that were listed in the charge, and one of the four even relates some of the same stories as *Newes from Ipswich* and calls Wren by the same epithet.[34] Yet Prynne was left instead to proclaim triumphantly that he could hardly make a defense when "there is no [one] book layd to my charge."[35] As for the authorship of the anonymous works, if it did really matter, the interrogatories administered under the Star Chamber oath could have secured this information. Star Chamber never took this trouble, however, because Prynne and Bastwick composed such fierce replies to the original information that their counsels would not sign their answers, while Burton's answer was cast out as impertinent, and all three men were then condemned *pro confesso* without ever being forced to volunteer any details of their activities.[36]

In effect, with their convictions a foregone conclusion anyway, The Triumvirate had tricked the Star Chamber into an action that deprived it of any benefit of interrogation and made its proceedings appear peculiarly arbitrary.[37] Prynne was able to point out that in Leighton's case seven years earlier the attorney general himself had moved that the court accept the defendant's answer under his own hand after his counsel refused to sign it, "least the defendant thereby excuse his contempt in not answering."[38] In 1630 the Star

Chamber had been anxious to let justice seem to be done and to learn from Leighton what it could. In 1637 its only aim was the speediest application of the most wholesome severity, and its members resorted to "an extraordinary kind of proceeding, more short and expeditious, which is called *ore tenus*," that is, judgment delivered orally without formal proof of guilt or any sort of testimony taken in writing beyond the confession of the accused. *Ore tenus* judgments made most sense in emergencies "when some dangerous persons attempt some unusual, and perhaps desperate inventions, which in short time may be very like to endanger the very fabric of government."[39] The use of the procedure in 1637 represents a kind of left-handed tribute to the seriousness with which the Star Chamber took the Triumvirate and its concomitant sense of crisis over the dangers posed by the Puritan opposition. Yet it would be hard to imagine a better way to give credence to the claims of that opposition than to take one of the most unpopular tactics of one of the highest of courts and misapply it totally to three men who claimed their only grievance was the Laudian episcopacy.

Under the best of circumstances judgments *ore tenus* were "much blamed as seeming to oppose the Great Charter, and other acts of Parliament," but their usual application did not entirely violate a rough sense of fair play. The Star Chamber proceeded without proof only when the defendant himself had previously provided it by a confession which he subsequently acknowledged at the bar before receiving sentence, while repudiation of the confession ordinarily required establishing of guilt in the usual way by written depositions from witnesses.[40] None of the Triumvirate, however, had actually confessed: they were merely proceeded against as if they had on the grounds that their answers were too scandalous to be admitted, even though the court could choose to punish con- tumacious answers by the familiar device of imprisonment for contempt.[41] The three men had set the bait by their answers and Star Chamber took it, bringing out perhaps the single most controver- sial weapon in its arsenal and using it in a blatantly inappropriate situation, so that injustice was clearly seen to have been done as publicly as possible. Instead of the confessed malefactors receiving the punishment appropriate to their crime and perhaps (in hope of mitigation) acknowledging the justness of their sentence them- selves, Star Chamber was left this time with three defendants dramatically protesting the very real failure to prove the case against them, and the downright unfairness of the whole trial.[42]

Judged in isolation the trial of 1637 appears the crowning instance of Laud's narrow-minded obsession with uniformity. Put in the perspective of the previous decade the same event becomes a misguided but understandable attempt at a drastic remedy by a man who had gradually come to think—with some show of reason—that he and his order were in imminent danger. Leighton's case had crystallized Laud's opinion, Prynne's first trial had reinforced it. With the censure of the Triumvirate Laud and the rest of the Star Chamber were just going through the same motions in triplicate. The information repeats the familiar charge that the libels brought government into disrepute, "tending to the raysinge of faction, and sedition amongst your people which otherwise would be obedient to your Majesty's government, and observe the settled discipline of the church," an accusation made more relevant in the case of *Newes from Ipswich* by actual rioting in the city in question.[43] Laud complained once more of the dangerous zeal of the English people, which the incendiaries hoped to ignite "and so to fire that unto a sedition in hope that they whom they causelessly hate, might miscarry in it." At one point in his speech even he realized he was refighting old battles and declined to elaborate on his assertion of the *jure divino* calling of episcopacy because "of this I have said enough, and in this place, in Leighton's case, nor will I repeat."[44]

Parallels with Leighton's case continued after the trial at the public mutilation of the three defendants. All three made "comfortable" addresses to the onlookers, comparing their sufferings to Christ's on Calvary by way of instruction.[45] It was widely assumed that Leighton would be sent into exile in some remote prison at the same time as the other three, and when the privy council investigated the popular demonstrations in support of the Triumvirate, James Ingram, the deputy warden of the Fleet, found it necessary to report that on the day before he was to take him to Caernarvon Castle Mrs. Leighton made William Prynne the gift of a beaver hat "which he refused."[46] Even after Bastwick, Burton, and Prynne were safely confined in their respective fortresses in August of 1637, their presumed confederate Leighton still seemed a threat while he enjoyed the relative liberty of a private apartment in the Fleet, free to treat patients and receive admiring visitors. Accordingly, in February of 1638, though Leighton had not written a line of controversy in eight years, on the report that he might be composing something new and keeping conventicles as well, he was inhibited from seeing visitors, removed from his private apartment, and thrown into the Fleet's common jail "amongst some sixteen or more of wicked and debased ones."[47] Then two months later, on 18 April 1638, when John Lilburne in the public pillory managed to scatter some antiepiscopal pamphlets, Deputy Warden Ingram complained that "there were old businesses rubbd up against me concerning *Dr. Laiton* and *Mr. Burton*."[48] Despite his long silence Leighton remained the prototypical boutefeu, the first link in an apparent chain of conspirators.

The paucity of evidence genuinely linking Leighton to the Triumvirate reduced propagandists to employing vague language to explain their association. All four were at least the same *sort* of men and very likely of the same "sect" or "brotherhood." Thus Christopher Dow's uneasy innuendo about Burton's true intentions towards the bishops:

> . . . perhaps he knows some intended mischiefe towards them, or hopes well that *his sermons* and the Ipswich Libell will worke so with some bloudy Assasines, that they may be brought (as his brother *Leighton* speaks) *to strike that Hazael* (the Bishops) *in the fift rib, to strike that Basilike vein, as the only cure for the plurises of this State.*[49]

The shadowy and apparently undiscoverable nature of the links between Burton, the author of the "Ipswich Libell," and Leighton had finally become proof positive of the sinister intentions of their presumed organization.

VI

RETROSPECT

The Dangers of Seditious Literature

IN DEFENSE OF LAUD and his allies it might be argued that however much they mistook particular details, they assessed their overall danger correctly. Though not actually a conspiracy, the authors of these libels and similar tracts brought the government into disrepute and incited the kind of insurrection which became a reality only a few years later. The survivors of the holocaust had the dubious satisfaction of knowing that subsequent events more than vindicated their darkest prophecies. Peter Heylyn among others spent several folios in later life making mainly this point, and in an age transfixed by the power of mass communications he seems believable enough. If the modern analogies are ignored for the moment, however, we are brought back to an interesting question: did the mechanics of the seditious book trade in the first half of the seventeenth century permit the kind of wide circulation of anti-government material that might constitute a real threat to the existing order in church and state?

The existing order never really asked this question: it assumed it knew the disposition of the people too well to bother. But enough evidence survives to piece together the rough outlines of the operation, which seems to have changed very little from the accession of

James I to the calling of the Long Parliament.[1] Finding a Dutch printer and smuggling his work back into England were the least difficult parts of the business, so that concentrating on these two aspects alone can inflate seditious printing into a very formidable problem indeed.[2] Actually, the stream of antigovernment material rode the tide of a much larger trade in pirated editions of religious and technical works made dear in England by the grant of exclusive printing rights to well-connected printers. The Dutch saw their opportunity to break these copyrights and took it for books in wide demand, especially the Geneva Bible.[3] Moxon at Rotterdam, who turned out one thousand copies of the *Letany*, simultaneously printed four thousand bibles and five thousand copies of the Psalms; Christiaans of Leyden, who incidentally turned out Bastwick's *Answer*, was similarly primarily a bible printer, as was Stam at Amsterdam, who had the capacity to undertake a contract for six thousand bibles at a single go.[4] After the bible, the most popular English works were probably pirated editions of the *Book of Common Prayer* and Lewis Bayly's *Practice of Piety*, a devotional work by a Welsh bishop of Puritan inclinations which had reached its forty-first reprinting by 1640.[5] By contrast, only a few of the genuinely seditious works achieved even one reprinting and although the size of their press runs is only occasionally recorded, the few times the number of copies printed is mentioned it falls between five hundred and a thousand copies. It was no wonder that when Stam received a contract for Geneva Bibles in 1633 his competitor, Staresmore, attempted to turn him in to the British ambassador: a man could not become much of a success at printing on six hundred copies of *Sions Plea*.[6] Prohibitive cost must have kept the press run of the less popular works small and necessitated either a personal sponsor or organizational subsidies, as in the case of the material turned out by the press of the Ancient Church.[7] When a commercial printer like Christiaans brought out one work at his own cost the English stationer Matthew Symmons drew special attention to the fact, though Christiaans could probably have financed the tract out of the profits of one of his pirated editions of William Lily's grammatical works.[8]

The existing trade in pirated books also made the smuggling of seditious literature comparatively easy. British merchants and sea captains trading between the Netherlands and England had gone into the book business as a sideline and over the years discovered ways to evade the customs men or to corrupt them. One customs officer in 1634 after seizing a contraband shipment of Common Prayer books offered, in return for a bribe, to "goe to Temple barre and buy a pairs of spectacles to see no further than the length of his Armc" and also to protect the smugglers from their competitors, "for that he had such intelligence as noe man els had."[9]

Once the books were in England, however, the difficulties really began. Sometimes they came over in small consignments, sometimes in relatively large ones, but as soon as they were in the country the shipments had to be broken down into very small lots (usually about one hundred books each) and distributed in a series of separate operations. Books which came over unbound to facilitate concealment were sent for stitching and then sale to stationers who might just decide to avoid risking trouble and turn their copies over to the High Commission. Stationers assumed to be sympathetic were chosen to receive the books, but there is no evidence of prior arrangement, and repayment to the original distributor, although occasionally attempted, was not really practical. At the very least, after selling off all the copies that would go quickly the bookseller could protect himself by turning in the rest.[10]

Alternatively, the shipments could be assigned to trustworthy amateurs for dispersal in still smaller lots, but these men would quickly find themselves facing very considerable risks. If they gave or sold their books only to trusted friends, they reached no one but the already converted;[11] if their copies went to men they were not sure of they placed themselves in the hands of a potential informer with every transaction. Many book transfers undoubtedly went undetected and still others were discovered without harm coming to the participants: the discrete and conformable minister or the well-affected layman might report suspicious goings on in his parish to a commissary or diocesan chancellor, but he had no guarantee that his complaint would be passed on to the privy council or High Commission. Nevertheless, the possibility of both detection and punishment was omnipresent, placing a definite limit on the freedom with which clandestine books could be circulated.

A Divine Tragedy and *Newes from Ipswich* were cases in point: the distributors did their work so energetically that most of them were eventually apprehended. Rice Boye, the Coleman Street Separatist, contacted one Edmund Chillington in October or November of 1636 "and asked him whether he could help him away with some bookes that he had of News from Ipswich and of the divine Tragedie that lay on his hands." Chillington, an apprentice button maker who eventually became a Fifth Monarchy Man, claimed to have connections at Norwich, whereupon Boye gave him fifty copies of each book. Chillington sent the whole lot to Edward Penton of Norwich, allegedly "a sanctified Brother, and [one who] hath bin already at New England," but a man whom Chillington knew of only by way of a third party. Nevertheless, Chillington forwarded this first shipment blind and even offered to send up more copies if Penton needed them, cautioning him, "but pray, be very warie." Penton was not: after selling off a large lot of the books to one buyer and scattering the rest he was arrested and to save himself informed on Chillington.[12] Interrogated in his turn, Chillington informed on Boye and for good measure gave evidence that helped to entrap John Lilburne, providing the latter with a good start as a popular martyr but terminating his short career as a secret agent.[13]

A true romantic could call such an organization a system of independent cells. Strip away the spy thriller trappings, however, and the clandestine book trade boils down to a hit-or-miss procedure that mostly missed. In order to reduce costs and make shipment safer seditious literature was always printed in relatively small quantities and was usually restricted to short tracts such as the most widely reprinted of all illegal works, the Lincolnshire *Abridgement* of 1605.[14] Risky and inefficient methods of distribution wasted a good portion of the already small press run, and only a minority of the remaining copies was likely to end up in the hands of potential converts to the cause: the other copies at most merely reinforced the convictions of readers who needed no converting. The exposure of any one copy could be increased, of course, by circulating it from hand to hand, but only if the readers were willing to run the same risks as the distributors: the first misjudgment broke the chain and probably brought about the capture of some of its members. This misadventure occurred to Nehemiah Wallington, the Eastcheap turner, in 1638 when he was called before the Star Chamber for possessing one copy each of *A Divine Tragedy, Newes from Ipswich,* and Burton's *Apology of an Appeale.* He had received one of the tracts from his brother and a second from "an unknowen party that brought them to my doore," and had passed on one of the three to a fellow turner, but then an acquaintance already in trouble with the Star Chamber turned in Wallington and his brother, along with several others, in hopes of getting off himself.[15]

The material could also be circulated anonymously by leaving it at the homes of influential persons or it could just be scattered in some public place (a favorite device with John Lilburne's prison "letters"). Neither tactic, however, was likely to build a mass constituency, and random scattering was better suited to squibs and broadsides than to even the shortest tract. All these techniques were essentially haphazard arrangements likely to create the maximum possible number of incidents with the minimum possible effect on public opinion.[16]

Unfortunately, the government of Charles I saw only the series of incidents without ever managing to piece them together into a realistic picture of the whole. As antiepiscopal tracts increased in vehemence and number after 1635 Archbishop Laud, ignorant of the details of their circulation, came to fear for his safety, and the government as a whole became more willing to consider stern measures to check the apparent erosion in the prestige of established authority. So serious a miscalculation while understandable was not inevitable: the exaggeration of the threat posed by Puritan propaganda is attributable less to a lack of solid information than to the intellectual rigidities and personal failings of the men charged with analyzing the information available.

The problem of improving the regulation of the printing trade fell in 1636 to the civil lawyer Sir John Lambe, who had gained a detailed if narrow knowledge of nonconformity and unlicensed printing from his service in various capacities in ecclesiastical courts, especially his office of dean of the arches for the province of Canterbury, and from membership on the High Commission.[17] Never more than a competent civilian at any time, age and routine had accentuated Lambe's singular inability to make connections. He treated every infraction before him as still another isolated manifestation of some ill-defined malady curable by common sense remedies, a deliberate aversion to method perhaps best illustrated by his handling of the case of Gregory Dexter.[18]

Dexter and William Taylor, both apprentice printers, appeared before the High Commission in 1637 for attempting to bring out William Prynne's *Instructions for Church Wardens* in the only known instance where Prynne resorted to an English press for one of his Tower works. The two young men pleaded poverty, made a full confession, and seem to have gotten off with little or no correction.[19] Lambe attributed this sort of activity on the part of young printers to financial desperation and he proposed as a remedy to exclude "strangers" from the printing trade while organizing a system of makework for *bona fide* journeymen printers out of their apprenticeship but unable to find employment.[20] Had he consulted his own list of London apprentices, prepared only the previous year, he might have noticed that Dexter and Taylor had been apprenticed to the firm of Widow Aldee, one of the printers of *Histriomastix* in 1632, when the two would have already been indentured.[21] So far from being an out-of-pocket innocent easily seduced by a little hard coin, Dexter was becoming a specialist in Puritan literature as opportunities allowed. In 1641 he entered into partnership with Widow Aldee's son (or son-in-law) and manager Richard Oulton, and together they brought out as their first work, John Milton's *Of Prelatical Episcopacy*. Other works of a similar nature followed regularly until 1644 when Dexter, on his own now, finally went too far with the first edition of Roger Williams's *The Bloudy Tenet* and joined Williams in Rhode Island.[22]

Sir John Lambe, of course, could not know the future but Dexter's case showed just how little interest he took in even the recent past. He was apparently uninterested in the one technical method of detection available to him, the use of typographical analysis to identify the delinquent presses, even though Dudley Carleton, a decidedly more sophisticated and talented servant of the crown, had employed it to track down the Brewer-Brewster press years before.[23] Arguably, not even Carleton in his prime would have conceived of dealing with Gregory Dexter by way of a criminal record, let alone a dossier on a suspicious character, but Lambe was no Carleton nor was he in his prime, and he carried his love of habitual routine to extraordinary lengths: the one major administrative attempt to deal with unlicensed printing, the Star Chamber decree of 11 July 1637, commits the full might of the state to regulating the wrong people.

The decree employs the classic remedies for discontent in a manner very much on the order of the privy council's efforts a few years earlier to avoid unrest in East Anglia during the dearth of 1629 by separating out for exemplary punishment the "lewde and dissolute persons" who "joyne themselves with the poore workmen to encrease theire disorders," while defusing the explosive potential of the latter group by various forms of makework.[24] Issued just one month after the trial of Burton, Bastwick, and Prynne, the 1637 regulations of the printing trade similarly make provision for keeping unemployed printers out of trouble by ensuring that they can find work. The decree also makes a small effort at cracking down on books smuggled in from abroad, but, still following Lambe's ideas, the majority of the new regulations are taken up with tightening controls over the London press by reducing the number of master printers and excluding individuals he had identified as known troublemakers.[25] As a method of dealing with sedition the decree is neither particularly original in conception nor particularly relevant to the problem at hand, since the overwhelming majority of the objectionable works were printed in the Netherlands and there is no clear evidence that any of the remainder were the product of the London press, with which the degree primarily concerns itself. Lambe in 1637 had simply assumed he was still dealing with the kind of men who regularly got in trouble with the High Commission ten years before and came up with an uninventive program combining paternalism with arbitrary punishment.

Given his rigorously unimaginative style of thinking, at least Lambe did not fall into the trap of overestimating the influence of the opposition to episcopacy, but neither did he ever understand its real nature or the manner in which its literary output might be controlled. Rather, Lambe's obsessive attention to the London stationers indicates his inability to comprehend the intricate network of personal relationships through which radical Puritan tracts were published and distributed. More or less by default, therefore, the task of scenting out the nature of the Puritan enemy fell mainly to Laud's chaplain, Peter Heylyn, a combative, clever young man who combined a fierce loyalty to his patron with a mania for system. William Lamont in an agreeably whimsical passage has described William Prynne as "the first modern historian: solemn, prolix and packed with footnotes." The title could go as easily to Heylyn, author of *Cosmographie in Four Books* and *A Help to English History*. He possessed, as well, a prodigious memory and an appetite for controversy, and he spent the last twenty years of his life vindicating the opinions he had enunciated in the first forty.[26] It was Heylyn who first extracted allegedly treasonable passages from Prynne's works in 1629, Heylyn who began an inquiry into the "Design" of the Feoffees for Impropria-

64

tions in 1630 and preached the opening attack on them, Heylyn who took notes on *Histriomastix* in 1632 and proceeded in 1633 "to deduct out of them such Logical Inferences and conclusions as might and did naturally arise on those dangerous Premises." His *History of the Sabbath* was conceived of and written simultaneously with Bishop White's *Defense of the Sabbath Day* in 1635, from which he picked up Leighton's allusion to Burton, and in 1637 it was Heylyn who prepared *A Moderate Answer* to Burton where he assessed the cause of the nonconformist problem: ". . . how have both Church and State been exercised by those factious Spirits, Layton and Prynne, and Bastwick, the Triumviri, with H. Burton and Dictator. . . ?"[27]

For Heylyn Puritanism was the English branch of the Presbyterian international, professing the least attractive dogmas of Calvin and Beza and dedicated to putting into effect the least attractive features of the Genevan model of church and state. Because of their tenets and their semi-illegal political status in every country in Europe, Presbyterians invariably fomented popular unrest under the color of spurious doctrines of contractual government, fundamental law, and the accountability of magistrates to church and commons.[28] Knox and Buchanan had incautiously revealed the true aims of their English brethren, while the cases of Leighton, et al. merely proved the proposition.

Where Lambe had displayed little inclination to put two and two together, Heylyn totaled the sum and came up with four conspirators. Together the two men so clouded over and distorted the nature of nonconformity that they made it easy for a desperate government, never very sure of itself in any case, to undertake the kind of ineffective and misdirected policy of repression which alone could alienate moderate opinion, create popular heroes out of extremists, and substantiate the wildest charges of its opponents. "By these devices, the Prelates hoped to have more prevailed; but it is feared they have lost greatly by it," the semiseparatist Henry Jacie noted with satisfaction in 1637, adding:

> the poor credit they had with the vulgar is almost quite lost. Every wrech, and swearing and drunken beast almost, is ready on the last speach, to cry out on them, which makes many consider Mal. 2. 8,9. Because you have caused many to stumble, ergo have I made you contemptible.[29]

VII

CONCLUSION

Whoso Diggeth a Pit . . .

THERE IS LITTLE POINT in improving on Peter Heylyn's original error by attributing not only the political unrest of the 1630s but also the outbreak of the Civil War to four Puritan polemicists. Rather, coming when he did, acting as he did, Alexander Leighton made some preconceptions seem more plausible than others, and his case thereby determined the cases of his successors, Bastwick, Burton, and Prynne, until they too "Leightonized" under pressure, fulfilling the original expectations of their prosecutors. After Leighton's case Laud was no more obliged to reject a "Presbyterian" plot as inconceivable than Prynne after his own first trial was required to doubt the existence of a popish one. The mutual suspicions so engendered received all the confirmation they might need after 1635 by the intensification of anti-Laudian propaganda on the one hand and of the Laudian regimen on the other. The resulting tensions helped to make the country so ungovernable in a time of crisis that the government of Charles I finally found itself falling back on the same ultimate remedy as its predecessors, the calling of a parliament. After November 1640, with Laud in prison and Prynne and the others on the outside, a wise and moderate course by all the leading parties arguably could have averted war, but the historical possibility of such an alternative has to be assessed against the resentments, fears, and expectations built up in the previous ten years as well as against the overall health of the body politic. Whatever the unfortunate effects of policy after 1630 there still had to be basic weaknesses in the fabric of the state which prevented it from withstanding the shock.

These qualifications said and done, the careers of all four men still possess an historical importance beyond their individual contributions to the Civil War, both in what they suggest about the policy of the Laudian Church and Caroline government in general, and, less obviously, in what they reveal about a portion of the Puritan movement with which Laud came into conflict. Because the authorities naturally kept better records than the "criminals," the primary emphasis in this discussion has accordingly gone to the reasons behind the exaggerated estimate of militant Puritanism and of its allegedly sinister intentions. But once we admit that despite the increasing involvement of the Caroline religious underground in clandestine printing it was never a cohesive network of revolutionary cells, that "crime," after all, was not particularly criminal, we may still find the men involved historically significant. Whatever their role in the coming of the Civil War, first and foremost their activities highlight the vitality and variety of Puritan religious life on the eve of the sectarian explosion of the Interregnum.

Up to a point the roots of this explosion lay in the 1630s when the pressure from above forced a considerable body of nonconformists, lay and clerical alike, to choose between their commitment to a national church and their participation in an increasingly militant Puritan underground of gathered conventicles. Prior to the Laudian ascendancy such an explicit choice had simply never been necessary. There were no official Puritan creeds to subscribe to as a precondition for friendly cooperation in the duties of Christian fellowship, and after the dissolution of the Classical movement in the 1590s formal organizations with formal rules became too dangerous. Instead, the private exercises that united the radicals depended only on association and habits of association built up by men such as Leighton and Bastwick over the course of a lifetime. Indeed, the real measure of religious radicalism, the one recognized as such by contemporaries before 1640, was not a man's putative preferences on the shape of discipline in some hypothetical re-

67

formed church of the future but the vigor with which he supported extraparochial activities and, sometimes, as in the cases of Bastwick and Leighton, the length of the spoon he would use to sup with the Separatists.

By this standard Burton originally only flirted with the radicals and Prynne's early attitude approached studied neutrality. But after Laud's hand had fallen upon them, and while they were simultaneously witnessing what they took to be the spread of popish and Arminian innovations in the English church, Prynne and Burton joined Bastwick and Leighton, edging considerably closer in practice to individuals whose views they had formerly suspected. The same curious and rather reluctant de facto separatism could be found on the parish level in the growing abstentionist practices of the Broadmead conventiclers and in the unhappy predicament spelled out by migrants to New England in the late 1630s when they tried to define their relationship to their ertswhile mother church in England. For example, one group from Rowley in Yorkshire, led by Ezekiel Rogers, had already, prior to their emigration in 1638, "of a good time withdrawn themselves from the church communion of England, and that for many corruptons which were among them." Rogers, a casualty of Richard Neile's translation to York, had been a longstanding clerical client of the important and eminently respectable Barrington clan of Essex and he had accepted episcopal ordination without even flirting with doctrinal Separatism. As spokesman for his people in 1638 he insisted that they all continued to acknowledge "a special presence of God there" amongst the remaining English Puritans, and yet "since God let them see some light therein, they could not with safe conscience join any longer with them . . . Hereupon they bewaled to the Lord their sinful partaking so long in these corruptons, and entered a covenant together to walk together in all the ordinances."[1] That is, they became Separatists in every respect except conscious choice.

In point of fact, the more cautious nonconformists did find private exercises coupled with abstention from the sacrament much too close to Separatism, with all that Separatism implied to them by way of popular and lay control of church affairs. The moderates found the practices of the radicals both a political embarrassment and a dangerously seductive alternative to the established ministry. The enthusiastic layman who avoided objectionable portions of the liturgy was not merely overzealous, he was also indirectly asserting that he shared some of the responsibility for church government with the official church governors. And so John Ball's critical observation, as condemnatory as anything from John Robinson or William Laud, on the nonconformist laity who refused the sacrament rather than participate in mixed communion:

> The main ground of the former doubt and all others tending to Separation seemeth to be this; That the power of the keys is primitively given to the community of the faithfull, as the first receptacle. For then they conceived that it pertaineth to them to censure offenders, or else to separate from them. Then likewise will it more probably be concluded, as they think, that the society which hath not the power of CHRISTS Keyes is not the true church of CHRIST.[2]

Ball was a genuine if conservative Puritan who had fallen afoul of episcopal authority himself for keeping private fasts. He died, however, in 1640 without seeing the issue of his strictures against lay initiative: they were published by two ministerial friends, who, under the guise of refuting Separatism and New England-bred deviations, used Ball's tracts to attack the newly emergent Independents in the name of a purified national church.[3] This great Puritan schism of the 1640s had an undeniable momentum of its own, originating in the disruptions of the Civil War and the problems of formulating an official credo for an opposition movement suddenly come to power, but some measure of the mutual hostility between Presbyterian and Independent derived from the 1630s, when for the first time radicals and moderates found their respective commitments irreconcilable. It may well be that despite his diminutive stature William Laud fits very well the role of a Caroline Samson, pulling down the temple on his enemies as well as himself.

In any event, Laud saw in radical Puritanism all the dangers that Ball had and more besides: a political threat to himself and to the state that could not be dealt with satisfactorily by ordinary legal procedures and that, maddeningly, despite its revolutionary aims failed to come within the bounds of the strict construction of the statute of treason. If this element of despairing defensiveness is added to the traditional picture of Laud the cocksure counter-revolutionary, then the archbishop himself becomes more plausible in his assault on nonconformity, more a man who thought he was fighting for survival and less one trying to do too much too soon. Undeniably, he had some disturbing changes planned for the Church of England and he was at once too rigid and too energetic in his attempts to enforce conformity to his ideal.[4] One may still doubt whether an individual singled out for so many administrative posts whose prime requisites were efficiency and discretion possessed either the inclination or the mental equipment to risk deliberately provoking massive opposition by contemplating a wholesale revolution. Neither at London nor at Canterbury did he attempt a purge of nonconformist ministers on a scale comparable to the ejections of 1662, and as Bishop of London, at least, he generally released Puritan clergymen on the mere pledge of future conformity.[5] His opponents may have thought he aimed at silencing all the exponents of orthodox doctrine, leaving only "Arminians" at liberty to preach, but he probably envisioned merely the conventional ideal of a land without divisive religious controversies. When Samuel Brooke offered to save England from the "Laytons" by his treatise against predestination Laud politely told him not to wake sleeping tigers:

> Nevertheless I am yet where I was, that something about these controversies is unmasterable in this life. Neither can I think any expression can be so happy as to settle all these difficulties. And however I do much doubt whether the King will take any man's judgment so far as to have these controversies any further stirred, which now, God be thanked, begin to be at more peace, etc.[6]

The man who welcomed the disastrous Star Chamber trial of 1637, who managed despite inherent judicial conservatism and personal animosities to get the rest of the court to follow his suicidal course, and who occasioned a score of lesser martyrdoms to fill in the case against him at his own impeachment, was hoping merely that a peculiarly vigorous use of customary police methods would eliminate a threat to church and state he had incorrectly inflated into a major menace because of a succession of unfortunate circumstances and his own perfectly ordinary assumptions about the true ends of Puritan political activity.

Laud was never noted for his sense of humor, and Peter Heylyn, who fancied himself a wit, never quite saw the joke in this particular situation either. The last laugh went instead neither to Laudian nor Puritan but to Archbishop John Williams, advanced at last to the see of York after it was too late to do him any good. When Williams read Laud's speech at the censure of Burton, Bastwick, and Prynne he took note that it began with a reference to his rival's many "diversions" in public service, and with a sarcasm made heavy by his own enforced leisure in the Tower the most politic churchman of the seventeenth century bequeathed to the age of marginalia perhaps the single most bitter of its many glosses:

> to neglect all Christian mildness and fall upon the killing and massacring of these poore flies in the Star Chamber, to draw malice and hatred upon all your coate and calling, was unto the Church of England a most unfortunate diversion. And doubt you not, but we shall consider and remember, as long as we live, your many Diversions.[7]

APPENDIX

The Propaganda Campaign

of 1636-37

Problems of Authorship and Provenance

THE SUCCESS OF THE Triumvirate in avoiding the Star Chamber oath may have been something of a master stroke on their part, but it has left later and more sympathetic students of their published work with a bibliographic tangle of formidable proportions. From the time of Laud to the present there have been repeated efforts to identify the authors and printers of the two most famous tracts, *A Divine Tragedy* and *Newes from Ipswich*, but progress always seems to go hand in hand with confusion because of the persistent tendency to award the composition of both works to Prynne, more or less by default, and because of the assumption, wholly unfounded, that at least some of the printing must have been done in England.

Newes from Ipswich is the more mysterious of the two. Never claimed for his own by any member of the Triumvirate, or by anyone else for that matter, the earliest known edition of the tract (STC 20470) also perversely calls itself "Edition 3" on the title page, while the text provides almost nothing by way of typographical evidence to help identify the printer. W. J. Couper clarified the history of the piece somewhat by establishing that a presumed earlier edition (STC 20469) is actually a *later*, Scottish reprint of the original, but he then attempted to account for the "missing" first two editions by suggesting that *Newes from Ipswich* was originally published simultaneously by three different English "provincial" presses.[1] Although echoed in some later studies, Couper's theory is rather fanciful.

1. Star Chamber decrees regulating English printing absolutely forbade any presses outside of London, except for those at the two universities.[2]

2. *Newes from Ipswich* did not lack for publicity, and if there really had been two other printings in 1636 besides "Edition 3" some mention of them would surely have survived. Yet only "Edition 3" is definitely known to have been in circulation in England by early 1637, while at least one contemporary observer doubted the existence of any other printings.[3]

3. The phrase "Edition 3" probably amounts to little more than a blind like the pseudonyms and false provenances similarly employed by Dutch presses to disguise their English work. The title page of Prynne's *Breviate* of 1637 (STC 20454) gives the author of the work as "W. Huntley, Esquirer," and also announces that the tract is a third edition, "much enlarged," despite the lack of any previous printing.

Having now been banished from the provinces, *Newes from Ipswich* could conceivably be reassigned to a London press, but this conjecture would encounter the same difficulties as the attempt to find a printer in the capital for the second edition of *A Divine Tradegy* (to be discussed below). The bulk of the Puritan propaganda of the 1630s originated in the Netherlands, and there is no particular reason to suppose *Newes from Ipswich* an exception, especially when the only available evidence (such as it is) points towards Amsterdam. Copies of the tract were distributed in England by Rice Boye, whose connections were all with the Dutch printer J. F. Stam, and the coranto format of the tract again suggests Stam because of the experience his firm had gained with English-language versions of that genre.[4] The total lack of ornaments, however, is not typical of Stam's English-language work, and there is an outside possibility that the tract is instead the work of the Ancient Church press, whose printers sometimes did employ rather anonymous typography.[5]

A Divine Tragedy poses some of the same problems as its sister work, but most of them can be resolved more definitively. At the least, the authorship of the main part of the work can be awarded to Henry Burton (and not to William Prynne).

1. Neither of the contemporary catalogues of Prynne's works lists the tract, while a reissue of 1641 (Wing STC B-6161) does identify Burton as the author.

2. Only a short time after the tract's first appearance Edward Rossingham reported that Burton admitted to writing all but the final section: "He [Burton] confesseth, as I hear, that he wrote the book, and gave it to a printer, who printed it against his knowledge; but he absolutely denieth that he wrote three or four leaves at the end of the book, which I hear, do very much scandalize Mr. Attorney Noy."[6]

The printer to whom Burton gave the work was presumably J. F. Stam again, who also brought out most of Prynne's prison works, and there is good reason to suspect Prynne's hand in *A Divine Tragedy*, but only in the one section disavowed by Burton. Of the two 1636 editions, the Stam imprint (STC 20459), is clearly the earlier of the two, using more elegant but far more imperfect typography and misordering the examples of divine judgment. In this edition the last piece has a different set of signatures from the rest of the work, indicating that it was hurriedly tacked on after the body of the text was complete. The substance of these final pages similarly does not have much to do with the rest of the text, dealing instead with Prynne's prosecution for *Histriomastix* from a point of view very decidedly Prynne's own. The inclusion of this matter in a collection of moral tales about sabbath breaking can best be explained by suggesting that as the imprisoned author of a series of fugitive tracts, Prynne would have to make his points when and where he could, even if necessary at the tail end of someone else's book which happened at that moment to be in the hands of his own printer.

Prynne's contribution to *A Divine Tragedy*, though minimal, is in a way responsible for an entire phantom printing house, the unknown London press credited by A. F. Johnson with bringing out the second edition of the tract along with second editions of two other works by Burton (the printer of the first editions was J. F. Stam in each case).[7] Any such press would constitute a remarkable exception to the contention that by the mid-1630s clandestine Puritan printing had become a virtual monopoly of the Netherlands, but Johnson's case rests almost entirely on a plausible misinterpretation of Prynne's one known effort during his imprisonment to enlist the services of a London printer.

The incident in question, however, is an anomaly, the unique product of Prynne's limited options combined with his passion for addenda, and nothing more. Of the London printers and stationers regularly patronized by Prynne and Burton between 1627 and 1633 or otherwise involved in circulating Puritan tracts, only Michael Sparke had anything like full freedom of operation left to him by 1636. The most radical of the lot, the bookseller James Boler (who had received shipments of William Ames' *Fresh Suit* from the Ancient Church press as late as 1633), had died in 1635, while the printers William Jones the younger and Augustine Matthews were in serious trouble with the authorities, and Matthews was ruined to boot. Jones was imprisoned for a time in 1636 and Matthews may have been also; both men were hurt still further the next year when they were left out of the list of authorized master printers under the new Star Chamber edict of 11 July 1637.[8] Prynne, therefore, had no familiar source to turn to for any of his last minute additions to the works he was turning out at high speed in the Tower, and in one instance he was forced to make use of what was left of his London connections by resorting, out of what was very probably desperation, to two apprentices of a firm that had printed a portion of *Histriomastix.* The sworn confessions of the two, Gregory Dexter and William Taylor, indicate only that on this occasion Prynne tried to get two of the numerous "epistles," appendices, and other odd items with which he delighted to adorn his works run off in London, not that the main portions of the texts themselves were ever produced there. Dexter and Taylor actually printed two distinct items: a) one thousand copies of *Brief Instructions to Church Wardens,* b) one thousand copies of the first four pages, five hundred copies of the second four pages, of part of a "scandalous epistle" to some larger work they neither pritned nor saw.[9] In order to throw the authorities off the scent, Prynne provided for the "epistle" a large initial "C" frequently used by Stam but not known in England, and as both editions of *A Divine Tragedy,* the second of unknown origin as well as the Stam imprint, use such a "C," Johnson, mistaking the exception for the rule, posited a London source for all of the second editions with identical typography. William Lamont subsequently took matters one step further and assigned the preface of *A Divine Tragedy* to Prynne for good measure, presumably on the basis of the epistle with the Dutch "C."[10]

Neither Dexter nor Taylor, however, could have had anything to do with *A Divine Tragedy*. The two apprentices swore under oath that they never saw the complete work for which their epistle was intended, yet the typography of both editions of *A Divine Tragedy* does not vary between the preface and the text, and in both editions the signatures are continuous. Additionally, the preface has nine pages, but the Dexter-Taylor "epistle" had only eight. The whole business merely proves that Prynne, true to his reputation, could not resist adding assorted extras to works already finished and that at least once he tried to get his additions printed up in London. *Brief Instructions* has no independent existence, and can only be found bound in at the end of the British Library's copy of Prynne's *Breviate of the Prelates Intolerable Usurpations* (shelf mark 698.1.46), which was printed by Stam. The unnamed "epistle" was probably also intended for some work printed in Holland and sent over unbound, although it may quite possibly have been destroyed before it could be added to the tract it was intended to complement. Thus, for example, another Prynne tract of Dutch origin, *The Lords Day the Sabbath Day*, promises "a Second Part and Postscript" on the title page while the preface apologizes for the omission of these additions because "some negligence and over-sight in the agents, hath frustrated both thine expectations and mine to."

If an individual printer must be found for the second editions of Prynne and Burton he had better be sought in the Netherlands. A tolerably good case (though no more) can be made for the most famous of English émigré printers, John Canne.

1. Canne was the legatee of the Ancient Church press after the departure of Staresmore from Amsterdam, and this press and Stam's had already printed duplicate editions of the same work in 1629 (Leighton's *Sions Plea*) and would do so again in 1637 and 1638.[11]

2. The typography of these second editions is not particularly revealing, but it does appear similar to that of the first editions, although cruder, a situation consistent with the known instances of

simultaneous imprints by Stam and the Ancient Church press.

3. Canne was residing in Amsterdam by 1634 and known to be printing Puritan polemics by 1637. Putting him into business one year earlier, in 1636, would certainly be the simplest and least objectionable solution to the problem of the second editions. While these works lack the characteristic "Richt Right" ornaments Canne eventually came to use on most of his known imprints, his products can not be isolated solely by distinctive typography. STC 22013, *News from Scotland* (Amsterdam, 1638) came from his press by his own confession, but it does not employ the "Richt Right" devices and it does use a large initial "C" not otherwise seen in his work. Again, Canne and Willem Christiaans of Leyden collaborated in 1637 on STC 11896, George Gillisepie's *A Dispute Against the English-Popish Ceremonies Obtruded upon the Church of Scotland,* yet it would be very difficult to tell their respective contributions apart.[12]

Canne or not, the probable source of the second edition of a work whose first edition came from a press in the Netherlands would be the proprietor of another press in the Netherlands. Nothing could have greater dramatic appeal than a hidden Puritan printer operating in London at full blast during the height of Laud's power, or, failing that, a string of daredevil apprentices of the Dexter stamp furtively cranking out seditious tracts by night on English commercial presses. But in sober fact most of the Puritan polemics of the 1630s are indisputably the work of printers in the Netherlands and not a single one of these tracts can be assigned to an English press with any degree of certainty.

NOTES

Notes to Chapter I

1. See below, note 51, chap. 2, and p. 53 and, for the Brewer Press, J. Rendel Harris and Stephen K. Jones, *The Pilgrim Press: A Bibliographical and Historical Memorial of the Books Printed at Leyden by the Pilgrim Fathers* (Cambridge, 1922).

2. Laud to Thomas Viscount Wentworth, 7 October 1637, *The Works of the Most Reverend Father in God, William Laud*, ed. W. Scott and J. Bliss, 7 vols. in 9 (Oxford, 1847-60), VII:373; John Williams, annotated copy of William Laud, *A Speech Delivered in the Starr-Chamber* . . . (London, 1788), sig. A2v.

3. For the varying use of the terms "Puritan" and "Nonconformist" see Perez Zagorin, *The Court and the Country: The Beginning of the English Revolution* (London, 1969), pp. 157-58. Of all modern historians Patrick Collinson has argued most forcefully and most persuasively against confusing lay Puritanism with clerical nonconformity and for the existence of a spontaneous, self-directed popular Protestantism: "The Godly: Aspects of Popular Protestantism in Elizabethan England" (Paper delivered at the *Past and Present* Conference on Popular Religion, 1966), p. 10; *The Elizabethan Puritan Movement* (Berkeley, 1967), pp. 372-81; "Towards a Broader Understanding of the Early Dissenting Tradition," in C. Robert Cole and Michael E. Moody, eds., *The Dissenting Tradition: Essays for Leland H. Carlson* (Athens, Ohio, 1975), pp. 3-38. See also R. C. Richardson, *Puritanism in North-West England: A Regional Study of the Diocese of Chester* (Manchester, 1972), chap. 3.

4. For episcopal attention to conventicles at Wolverhampton between 1630 and 1635 see the case of William Pinson, PRO, SP 16/388, fols. 182-92; for Northamptonshire in 1638, the case of Miles Burkett, PRO, SP 16/406, fol. 178 r. Bishop William Pierce of Bath and Wells suppressed the market day lecture at Taunton in 1637 because "it is the occasion of conventicles, for many cloake their secret meetings in this kind under a Pretense of Market business." Pierce to Laud, 6 October 1637, Lambeth Palace Library, MS 943, p. 563. It should be noted that neither Pinson, an attorney, nor Burkett, an inconformable minister, were accused of outright Separatism and that most of the "conventicles" in question were simply private fasts, prayer meetings, or unauthorized lectures. The word "conventicle" simply meant any private religious gathering attended by more than the house-holder's immediate family, a definition used by Laud in 1631 and repeated in the 1634 investigation into the affairs of John Angell, town lecturer of Leicester, where the eighth of eight interrogatories read, "Doth he not somtymes keepe conventicles in his owne or anie other house, that is, doth he not expounde holy scripture, and make prayers of his owne more beinge present then his owne households?" For Angell's case, see SP 16/540, fol. 344; for Laud's opinion, see Samuel Rawson Gardiner, ed., *Reports of Cases in the Courts of Star Chamber and High Commission*, Camden Society, n. s., XXXIX (London, 1886), pp. 140-41.

5. Gardiner, *Cases in the Courts of Star Chamber and High Commission*, p. 212.

6. Christopher Dow, *Innovations Unjustly Charged Upon the Present Church and State* (London, 1637), pp. 198-200.

7. Roger Hayden, ed., *The Records of a Church of Christ in Bristol, 1640-1687*, Bristol Record Society, XXVII (Bristol, 1974), pp. 83-91.

8. John Eliot to Richard Baxter, 7 October 1657, in Frederic James Powicke, ed., *Some Unpublished Correspondence of the Reverend Richard Baxter and the Reverend John Eliot . . .* (Manchester, 1931), pp. 24-25. Eliot was referring to his life at Chelmsford "before I came to N.[ew] E.[ngland] in the BBs [Bishops'] times." Cf. Geoffrey Nuttall, *Visible Saints* (Oxford, 1957), p. 83, who suggests that Hooker's association may have met at Little Baddow rather than Chelmsford.

9. For the group at Boston see John Cotton's letter to Samuel Skelton, 2 October 1630, *William and Mary Quarterly*, 3d. ser., XXII (1965):484 (from which the quotation comes) and his statement in *The Way of Congrega-tional Churches Cleared: In Two Treatises* (London, 1648), p. 20. Thomas Weld, one of Hooker's associates at Chelmsford and sometime minister of Terling, wrote his former parishioners in 1633 that in New England "we pray for your congregations publique and prived . . ." (British Library, Sloane MS 922, fol. 93 r.). John Vicars, minister of Stamford, was articled against in the High Commission in 1631 for (among other things) keeping conventicles and drawing off a part of his congregation into a covenanted inner church under the pretense of preparing them for the sacrament. His defense virtually accepts the charge of conventicling and makes no reply on the subject of a special covenant. At Vicar's sentencing Laud (probably thinking of John White of Dorchester) made his observation about the

West of England. (Gardiner, *Cases in the Courts of Star Chamber and High Commission*, pp. 198-99, 200, 202, 206, 215-16, and 218.)

10. *A Treatise of the Lawfulness of Hearing of the Ministers in the Church of England, The Works of John Robinson*, ed. Robert Ashton, 3 vols. (London, 1851), III:475-78.

11. John Cotton, "Letter of Mr. John Cotton, and Roger Williams' Reply," ed. Reuben A. Guild, in *The Complete Writings of Roger Williams*, Publications of the Narragansett Club, I (Providence, 1866) p. 309. Cotton's rejoinder to Williams's reply indicates that "Conventicles of the puritans" refers to "their frequent and continually meetings to duties of humiliation." (Ibid., II:190.)

12. Perry Miller, *Orthodoxy in Massachusetts, 1630-50: A Genetic Study* (Cambridge, Mass., 1933), chap. 4; Champlin Burrage, *The Early English Dissenters in the Light of Recent Research (1550-1641)*, 2 vols. (Cambridge, 1912), I:chaps. 12-14. Subsequent criticisms of the concept of "nonseparating congregationalism" are summarized in Collinson, "Towards a Broader Understanding of the Early Dissenting Tradition," pp. 7-10.

13. John Bellamie, *A Justification of the City Remonstrance and its Vindication* (London, 1646), pp. 29-30; John Price, *The City Remonstrance Remonstrated, or an Answer to Colonell J. Bellamy* (London, 1646). p. 18. Cf. the very similar exchange between John Goodwin and William Prynne cited below, n.16, chap. 2. For Bellamie see below, n.34 chap.2.

14. Arthur Hildersham, *CVIII. Lectures Upon the Fourth of John* (London, 1632), p. 253; cf. Richardson, *Puritanism in North-West England*, pp. 83-85.

15. Harley Papers, British Library, Loan 29/172, fols. 251-52. The "Queries" are not in Harley's handwriting but they are clearly Puritan in origin: they also propose resurrection of the Feoffees for Impropriations, confiscation of episcopal revenues, abolition of all cathedral chapters, and the passage of a strict sumptuary law. For Harley's part in one notorious private fast see below, n. 14, chap. 2. His importance to the Puritan movement before 1640 is discussed in Paul S. Seaver, *The Puritan Lectureships: The Politics of Religious Dissent, 1560-1662* (Stanford, 1970), pp. 49-52. See also Richardson, *Puritanism in North-West England*, pp. 86-97.

16. The conversion narratives of John Stedman and Edward Collins, taken down at the time of their admission to the church of Cambridge by its minister Thomas Shepard under the title "The Confessions of those Propounded to be Received and [who] were Entertayned as members." The original record is transcribed in its entirety (with modernized spelling) in Bruce C. Woolly, "Reverend Thomas Shepard's Cambridge Church Members, 1636-1649: A Socio-Economic Analysis" (Ph.D. diss., University of Rochester, 1973), the quoted passages occurring on pp. 115 and 122 respectively.

17. Hildersham, *CVIII. Lectures*, p. 254.

18. British Library, Add. MSS, 4275, fol. 289. The three ministers are John Cotton, Richard Bernard, and Francis Higginson (for his career at Leicester see below, n. 21, chap. 2).

19. Hildersham, *CVIII. Lectures*, pp. 129, 130-31.

20. Robinson, *Works*, II:101; John Smyth, *The Works of John Smyth*, ed. W. T. Whitley, 2 vols. (Cambridge, 1915), II:332; Ronald A. Marchant, *The Puritans and the Church Courts in the Diocese of York, 1560-1640* (London, 1960), p. 151; B. R. White, *The English Separatist Tradition: From the Marian Martyrs to the Pilgrim Fathers* (Oxford, 1971), pp. 111, 122. Richard Baxter similarly organized private meetings of members of his Kidderminster congregation in the 1650s on the grounds that "if I had not allowed them such as were lawful and profitable, they would have been ready to run to such as were unlawful and hurtful." *Reliquiae Baxterianae* (London, 1696), p. 88.

21. Albert Peel, ed., *The Seconde Part of a Register: Being a Callendar of Manuscripts . . . Intended for Publication by the Puritans about 1593*, 2 vols. (Cambridge, 1915), II:44-45.

22. From Cotton's letter to unnamed friends, quoted in Robert Baillie, *A Dissuasive from the Errours of the Time* (London, 1646), pp. 66-67. The authenticity as well as the date of the letter are established in Cotton, *Way of Congregational Churches*, pp. 28-29; Robert Baillie, *The Disswasive from the Errors of the Time, Vindicated From the Exceptions of Mr. Cotton and Mr. Tombes* (London, 1655), pp. 14-16.

23. British Library, Sloane MS 922, fols. 92v., 93r. The "men of Gibea" is an allusion to Judges 19: 22-30.

24. Stephen Dennison, *The White Wolfe; Or, a Sermon Preached at Pauls Crosse, Feb. 11 . . . Anno 1627* (London, 1627), pp. 20-21. The tract is an attack on a lay conventicle keeper, John Hetherington (or Etherington), incorrectly and abusively charging him with "Familism." Cf. *The Defence of John Etherington against Stephen Denison* (London, 1641), pp. 7-8 and *passim*, and for Dennison (or Denison), Seaver, *Puritan Lectureships*, pp. 144-45, 347n., 370n.

25. John Davenport, *Letters of John Davenport, Puritan Divine*, ed. Isabel MacBeath Calder (New Haven, 1937), p. 24. For the context of this exchange see below, pp. 18-19, and for Davenport's early conformity (abandoned abruptly in 1633 or 1634) see ibid., pp. 13-16, 19, 33-38; Isabel MacBeath Calder, *The New Haven Colony* (New Haven, 1934), chap. 1.

26. Hayden, *Records of a Church of Christ*, pp. 83 ff. Cf. Nuttall, *Visible Saints*, p. 48n.2. The Welsh preachers included William Wroth and Walter Cradock, for whom see ibid., p. 341 and *passim*.

27. Samuel Collins (minister of Braintree) to Dr. Arthur Duck, 20 May 1629, SP 16/142, fol. 239r. See also H. R. Trevor-Roper, *Archbishop Laud, 1573-1645*, 2d ed. (London, 1962), pp. 118-19.

28. For Laud's confusion over "Anabaptists" and "Presbyterians" see his *Works*, I:82-83. Directly after the trial of some *antinomians* in the High Commission in 1632 he ordered Prynne "articled against for the same; we must not sitt heere to punish poore snakes, and lett him goe scotfree." (Gardiner, *Cases in the Courts of Star Chamber and High Commission*, pp. 271, 314.)

29. See for example Peter Heylyn, *Cyprianus Anglicus: Or the History of the Life and Death of . . . William . . . Archbishop of Canterbury*

(London, 1668), p. 469 where the author has an "Anabaptist" congregation in 1640 and 1641 (probably the Jacob church, which was not yet, in fact, Baptist) denying obedience first to "Bishops' laws" and then any law of Charles I because he was *"not PERFECTLY REGENERATE, and was only to be obeyed in Civil Matters."* Heylyn may have had in mind the bizarre Hacket-Copinger case in the reign of Queen Elizabeth (see Collinson, *Elizabethan Puritan Movement*, pp. 424-25). Laud expressed similar views in his "Answer to Lord Say's Speech Touching the Liturgy," *Works*, VI:132-33.

30. Giles Widdowes, *The Lawlesse Kneelesse Schismaticall Puritan* (Oxford, 1631), p. 7. This argument in various forms is also the burden of much of Peter Heylyn's work, especially *Aerius Redivivus: Or the History of the Presbyterians . . . From the Year 1536 . . . to 1647* (Oxford, 1670). Cf. Francis White, *A Treatise of the Sabbath-Day* (London, 1635), preface; Collinson, *Elizabethan Puritan Movement*, p. 462.

31. Laud, *Works*, VI:234-35. At Leighton's initial interrogation before the High Commission the civilian Thomas Ryves also made the stock analogy between his activities and those of the Jesuits. Alexander Leighton, *An Epitome of Briefe Discoverie . . . of the . . . Great Troubles that Dr. Leighton Suffered in his Body, Estate, and Family* (London, 1646), p. 10.

Notes to Chapter II

1. George Gerrard to Edward Viscount Conway, ca. July 1637, quoted *verbatim* in *Calendar of State Papers, Domestic Series, Charles I, 1637*, p. 344; White, *Treatise of the Sabbath Day*, sig. ***3r; Leighton, *An Epitome*, p. 67; Smectymnuus [pseud.], *A Vindication of the Answer to the Humble Remonstrance* (London, 1641), pp. 216-17.

2. One qualification should be added: the British Museum *General Catalogue of Printed Books* awards Leighton the authorship of an anonymous tract of 1642, *King James his Judgment of a King and of a Tyrant*. The author does allude to himself as a Scot and an equally anonymous reply calls him "english bred" and "either Brownist, Anabaptist, or Separatist." *King Charles his Defence Against Some Trayterous Observations Upon King James his Judgement of a King and of a Tyrant* (London, 1642), p. 2. Both circumstances support Leighton's authorship of the former tract, which is, in turn, one of the earliest calls for the deposition of Charles I, but I can find no other corroborating evidence to confirm the attribution.

3. Leighton's *Epitome* does not refer to the Civil War nor to his own appointment as keeper of Lambeth House prison and it treats the continuation of episcopacy as a live issue, which suggests that it was composed about 1641 and then published some five years later to support a petition for

compensation then before the House of Lords and calendared in Historical Manuscripts Commission, *Sixth Report* (London, 1877), p. 158b. under the date of 13 February 1646/47.

4. Leighton's date of birth is unknown; he claimed (*An Epitome*, p. 91) to be almost seventy-two in 1640, putting the year of his birth about 1568, but the age he gave on the entry roll at Leyden would make it 1577, while the description of him in the proclamation for his arrest in 1630 makes him younger still.

5. For Leighton at Newcastle see John Brand, *The History and Antiquity of the Town and County of the Town of Newcastle upon Tyne*, 2 vols. (London, 1789), I:321, 323, 375, 412n.; Samuel Rawson Gardiner, *History of England from the Accession of James I to the Outbreak of the Civil War, 1603-1642*, 10 vols. (London, 1884-86), VII:vi. An "Alex. Lighton" served as a Newcastle curate as far back as 1586, suggesting we may not be dealing with the same man in every instance, but the Newcastle connection of the Puritan pamphleteer is confirmed in a letter of 1639 (SP 16/413, fol. 66r). For Leighton at the University of Leyden, and his putting up at Brewer's along with Bastwick, see Daniel Plooij, *The Pilgrim Fathers from a Dutch Point of View* (New York, 1932), p. 83.

6. Harris and Jones, *Pilgrim Press*, chap. 2; Plooij, *Pilgrim Fathers*, chap. 3.

7. Burrage, *Early English Dissenters*, I:202-03; Edward Arber, ed., *The Story of the Pilgrim Fathers, 1606-1623 A.D.* (London, 1897); Thomas Brewer, *Gospel Publique Worship* (London, 1656). The prophecy of the two kings is obviously taken from the eleventh chapter of Daniel.

8. The quotation comes from the High Commission proceedings against Bastwick on 12 February 1635 (SP 16/261, fol. 178v).

9. John Bastwick, *The Second Part of the Book Call'd Independency Not Gods Ordinance* (London, 1645), sigs. A3r.-A4r., Thomason Tract E.287.(9). Bastwick's life at Colchester and his trial before the High Commission are discussed below, pp. 47-48.

10. Leighton was inhibited by the Board of Censors of the College of Physicians on four separate occasions, the last while he was in prison: 24 September 1619, 7 July 1626, 5 January 1627, and 18 February 1634 (Gardiner, *History of England*, VII:vi). Not even the last injunction interfered with his practice despite his continued confinement.

11. Alexander Leighton, *An Appeal to the Parliament, or Sions Plea Against the Prelacie* (Amsterdam, 1628 [i.e., 1629]), pp. 34-35; Leighton, *An Epitome*, pp. 6-10.

12. Alexander Leighton, *Speculum Belli Sacri; Or the Looking-Glasse of the Holy War* (Amsterdam, 1624), pp. 206-07.

13. The significance of fast and feast days, and of the ensuing conflict over them, is discussed in Horton Davies, *Worship and Theology in England from Andrewes to Baxter and Fox, 1603-1690* (Princeton, 1975), chap. 6, especially pp. 245-49.

14. George Montaigne, Bishop of London, to the Duke of Buckingham, 12 December 1626, SP 16/525, fol. 48, reprinted in Raymond P. Stearns, ed., "Letters and Documents by or Relating to Hugh Peter," *Essex Institute*

Historical Collections, LXXII (1936):7-8. Montaigne claimed that Sir Robert Harley and the Earl of Warwick sponsored Peter's sermon, while Warwick subsequently observed, "and that which I grieve is most carpet [carped] at is that men kept a fast that day" (that is, St. Andrew's Day). (Warwick to Peter, n.d., ibid., pp. 8-9.) For Burton's sermon see below, p. 50.

15. Robert Ryece (the Suffolk Antiquary) to John Winthrop, 9 September 1636, *The Winthrop Papers,* ed. Massachusetts Historical Society (Boston, 1929-   ), III:306. See also Laud, *A Speech Delivered in the Star Chamber . . . , Works,* VI:46-47.

16. John Goodwin, *Certaine Briefe Observations and Antiquaeries: on Master Prin his Twelve Questions About Church Government* (London, 1644), p. 7, Thomason Tracts E.10.(33); William Prynne, *A Full Reply to Certain Brief Observations* (London, 1644), p. 10; Nehemiah Wallington, *Historical Notices of Events . . . in the reign of Charles I,* ed. R. Webb, 2 vols. (London, 1864), I:132-33. The Lambeth Palace riot of 11 May 1640 was immediately preceded by several weeks of intensive organization of these private meetings, indoor and outdoor, to pray for the continuation of the Short Parliament. See Valerie Pearl, *London and the Outbreak of the Puritan Revolution: City Government and National Politics, 1625-43* (London, 1961), pp. 107-08; Burrage, *Early English Dissenters,* II:300-10.

17. SP 16/175, fol. 178r (Laud labelled this unsigned paper "The City Censures concerning Leightons escape"). A meeting of the Jacob church was apprehended at a house in Blackfriars in 1632. (Gardiner, *Cases in the Courts of Star Chamber and High Commission,* pp. 278-79.)

18. For Goodyear (who had left England with Bastwick in 1616 and entered the University of Leyden with him in 1617) see Keith L. Sprunger, "Other Pilgrims in Leiden: Hugh Goodyear and the English Reformed Church," *Church History,* XLI (1972):46-60.

19. The Smith letter is reprinted in full in Plooij, *Pilgrim Fathers,* p. 92. For John Wing see Burrage, *Early English Dissenters,* I:313-15, II:293n. Wing was in Holland as early as 1621 as a charter member of the English classis there, but in 1619 Sabine Staresmore, Leighton's printer, speaks of consulting Wing and John Dod, another backer of Jacob's church, over the lawfulness of Common Prayer. (Sabine Staresmore, *The Unlawfulness of Reading in Prayer* [Amsterdam, 1619], pp. 27-28.) For Hugh Peter's early career in London and the Netherlands see Ramond P. Stearns, *The Strenuous Puritan: Hugh Peters, 1598-1660* (Urbana, Ill., 1954), pp. 35-44 and chap. 3 *passim.* At Amsterdam Peter fell into the embarrassing habit of attending Brownist meetings. Cf. John Davenport, *An Apologeticall Reply to a Booke Called an Answer to the Unjust Complaint of W. B.* (Rotterdam, 1636), p. 61.

20. For Smith in general see Plooij, *Pilgrim Fathers,* chap 4. Smith, an inconformable minister, spoke of himself as having had to make "18 removalls in 6 yeres" on both sides of the Atlantic because of his "persecuted condition." (Ibid., p. 114.) The Massachusetts Bay Company certainly was dubious about the "distraccion" his opinions might cause in their Salem Colony in 1629, but the earliest ascription of outright Separa-

tist principles to Smith dates from a history of Massachusetts written in 1682, long after his death. (Nathaniel B. Shurtleff, ed., *Records of the Governor and Company at the Massachusetts Bay in New England*, 5 vols. [Boston, 1853-54], I:390; William Hubbard, *A General History of New England, From the Discovery to MDCLXXX*, ed. William T. Harris [Boston, 1848], p. 97.)

21. Hildersham's associate at Leicester was Francis Higginson, for whom see Cotton Mather, *Magnalia Christi Americana; Or the Ecclesiastical History of New England*, 2 vols. (Hartford, Conn., 1853), I:357. The Leighton-Angell episode may be found in SP 16/178, fols. 128-32. The quotation is at fol. 131v.

22. Leighton, *Sions Plea*, pp. 6-7. Cf. the statement in the Cambridge Platform (indirectly derived from Thomas Cartwright) in Williston Walker, ed., *The Creeds and Platforms of Congregationalism*, paperback ed. (Boston, 1960), pp. 217-18, 218n.1.

23. Leighton, *Sions Plea*, pp. 330-33.

24. A. F. Johnson, "The Exiled English Church at Amsterdam and its Press," *The Library*, 5th ser., V (1950-51):238-39.

25. The mechanics of the Dutch trade will be discussed in greater detail below, pp. 59-60. There is no account of clandestine English printing that is both complete and comprehensive but Leona Rostenberg attempts a beginning in *The Minority Press and the English Crown: A Study in Repression, 1558-1625* (Niewkoop, 1971), especially chap. 15. There are, however, canons for individual presses, which taken collectively and in conjunction with manuscript evidence permit some generalization, though all studies of particular printers rely too heavily on identification by typography in a period when typefaces and ornaments were widely shared. The work of A. F. Johnson is particularly outstanding: in addition to "The Exiled English Church at Amsterdam and its Press" see his "J. F. Stam, Amsterdam, and English Bibles," *The Library*, 5th ser., IX (1954):185-93, and "Willem Christiaans, Leyden, and his English Books," ibid., X (1955):121-23. See also Harris and Jones, *Pilgrim Press* and J. Dover Wilson, "Richard Schilders and the English Puritans," *Transactions of the Bibliographical Society*, XI (1909-11):65-134.

26. Walter Wilson Greg, ed., *A Companion to Arber* (Oxford, 1967), pp. 226-29 (the quotation is taken from p. 228). For the authors of this literature cf. Louis B. Wright, "Propaganda Against James I's 'Appeasement' of Spain," *Huntington Library Quarterly*, VI (1942-43): 149-72; S. L. Adams, "Captain Thomas Gainsford, the 'Vox Spiritus' and the *Vox Populi*," *Bulletin of the Institute of Historical Research*, XLIX (1976):141-44; Jerry H. Bryant, "John Reynolds of Exeter and his Canon: A Footnote," *The Library*, 5th ser., XVIII (1963):299-303.

27. Alexander Leighton, *A Friendly Triall of the Treatise of Faith* (Amsterdam, 1624), pp. 2-3. For Culverwell's attempt to satisfy Leighton privately see *A Briefe Answer to Certain Objections Against the Treatise of Faith*, sigs. A3r.-v. in *A Treatise of Faith*, 8th ed. (London, 1646-48).

28. The account of Staresmore that follows is based on Burrage, *Early English Dissenters*, I:171-82, with certain amplifications, additions, and

corrections noted at the appropriate places. For the militant Puritans in the Netherlands in general see Keith L. Sprunger, *The Learned Doctor William Ames: Dutch Backgrounds of English and American Puritanism* (Urbana, Ill., 1972), chap. 10.

29. *The Visitation of the County of Leicester in the Year 1619*, Publications of the Harleian Society, II (1870):6.

30. For the Jacob church and its influence see Miller, *Orthodoxy in Massachusetts*, pp. 75ff; Nuttall, *Visible Saints*, pp. 10-11, 34; Burrage, *Early English Dissenters*, I:chap. 13. Staresmore describes his break with his mentor, Richard Maunsell, in his *Unlawfulness of Reading in Prayer*. For Maunsell's earlier involvement in radical activities see below, n. 35.

An important reconsideration of the nature and influence of the Jacob church is provided by Murray Tolmie, *The Triumph of the Saints: The Separate Churches of London, 1616-1649* (New York, 1977). Tolmie's work unfortunately appeared too late to be more than noted in this study.

31. Burrage, *Early English Dissenters*, I:174, places Staresmore's first entry into the Leyden church in 1623 or 1624 *after* his excommunication from Amsterdam; Robinson, however, makes clear in a letter of 18 September 1624 to the Ancient Church that Staresmore's *initial* admission into Amsterdam was by way of Leyden. (*Works*, III:390-91.) Moreover, Staresmore was already acting as an agent in London for the Leyden church and calling several of its members "brother" as early as 1618. William Bradford, *History of Plymouth Plantation, 1620-1647*, 2 vols. (Boston, 1912), I:82-83, 92-94.

32. Burrage, *Early English Dissenters*, I:175-77, incorrectly has Staresmore in charge of a fully covenanted rival Amsterdam Separatist church between 1624 and 1630. The passages Burrage quotes from A. T., *A Christian Reprofe Against Contention* (Amsterdam, 1631), pp. 15ff., 40ff. (STC 23605), refer to the Jacob and Leyden churches respectively and not to some third congregation run by Staresmore. In his own defense in 1630 Staresmore does declare that "notwithstanding all this, the Lord in mercy hath here raysed another church void of these scandals that walk in the fear of God," presumably an allusion to the new ministry of John Canne at the original Ancient Church. (Henry Ainsworth, *Certain Notes of M. Henry Aynsworth His Last Sermon* [Amsterdam, 1630], marginal note in the unpaged "Postscript." This tract is STC 227.)

33. Burrage, *Early English Dissenters*, I:182. Burrage apparently was unaware of Staresmore's role in the Davenport-Paget controversy: Staresmore printed (and in Paget's eyes helped devise) William Best's *A Just Complaint Against an Unjust Doer* (Amsterdam, 1634). He also gave the work its title and an inflammatory postscript, p. 24, advising the Davenport party that *"the way of the upright is to depart from evill."* See John Paget, *An Answer to the Unjust Complaints of William Best* (Amsterdam, 1635), sigs. (*)2v., 3v. For good measure Staresmore showed the Best tract to Paget while it was still in press, allowing the latter time to compose his reply. See Davenport, *An Apologeticall Reply*, sig. (⁎⁎) 3v. For the whole controversy cf. Alice C. Carter, *The English Reformed Church in Amsterdam in the Seventeenth Century* (Amsterdam, 1964), pp. 81-83; Calder, *New Haven Colony*, pp. 22-28.

34. For Staresmore in 1646 see Bellamie, *Justification of the City Remonstrance*, pp. 21-22, and for the Remonstrance itself see Valerie Pearl, "London's Counter Revolution," in G. E. Aylmer, ed., *The Interregnum: The Quest for Settlement* (London, 1972), pp. 35ff. Staresmore's role in the Leveller petition is described in William Walwyn, *Walwyn's Just Defense Against . . . a . . . Pamphlet Entitled Walwyns Wiles* (London, 1649), p. 4. For the conference on the fate of the Southwark church in 1644 see *Transactions of the Baptist Historical Society*, I (1910):243. Those present at the meeting on 27 March 1644 were: "Mr. Barbone, Rozer [i.e., Rogers], Dr. Parker, Mr. Erbury, Mr. Cooke, Mr. Thomas Goodwin, Mr. Phillip Nye, Mr. G. [*sic*] Sympson, Mr. Burrowns, Mr. Staismore."

35. Staresmore was involved with several individuals prior to 1623 who could have provided him with his initiation. Both Richard Maunsell and Henry Jacob had a hand in a venture in clandestine printing in 1608-09, and John Bellamie, another early member of the Jacob Church, became a London bookseller with Leyden connections and, later, a prominent figure in London politics during the Civil War. See Mark H. Curtis, "William Jones: Puritan Printer and Propagandist," *The Library*, 5th ser., XIX (1964):38-66; Pearl, "London's Counter Revolution," pp. 33ff., and the same author's *London and the Outbreak of the Puritan Revolution*, pp. 137, 152; Leona Rostenberg, *Literary, Political, Scientific, Religious and Legal Publishing, Printing and Bookselling in England, 1551-1700: Twelve Studies* (New York, 1965), pp. 98ff. Equally, Staresmore's stay in Leyden suggests a tie to Brewer, and his translation to the Amsterdam Separatist church about 1622 coincides almost exactly with the first use of "Pilgrim Press" ornaments and types by the press of the Ancient Church. See Johnson, "The Exiled English Church," pp. 230-32.

36. For Thorpe see Johnson, "The Exiled English Church," p. 220. Johnson suggests Thorpe died shortly after the church's minister, Henry Ainsworth, a point confirmed by Staresmore in *Certain Notes of M. Henry Aynsworth His Last Sermon*, "A Postscript to the Brethren Absent" (unpaged). The quotation comes from William Best in "The Churches Plea for Due Liberty," British Library, Add. MSS, 24, 666, fol. 34v. The next year Paget called Staresmore simply "The Printer of the Brownists," while he is named in 1633 as the printer of William Ames's *A Fresh Suit Against Human Ceremonies in Gods Worship* (Amsterdam, 1633), which is definitely an Ancient Church production. Paget, *An Answer to the Unjust Complaints of William Best*, sig. (*) 2v.; Greg, *Companion to Arber*, p. 292; Johnson, "Exiled English Church," p. 241. The date of Staresmore's assumption of control of the press, however, is not quite so clear: *The Loving Tender*, and consequently its identifying typography have been lost, while the name of Richard Playters appears on some Ancient Church work, and Johnson even attributes the anti-Staresmore blast of 1631, *A Christion Reprofe*, to the press. Staresmore himself, however, dates *The Loving Tender* at 1623 (*Certain Notes*, "Postscript"), while "A. T." observes that both it *and* the *Certain Notes* of 1630 (which is undoubtedly an Ancient Church book) come from Staresmore's "Printery." *A Christian Reprofe*, p. 3. Either the Ancient Church Press types were divided in 1623,

or Staresmore shared the work with Playters; certainly, he had control of at least part of the press from that year. As for *A Christian Reprofe*, only its subject allowed Johnson to assign it to the Ancient Church press rather than to J. F. Stam or some other Amsterdam printer (its typography is not typical of other Ancient Church publications).

37. Randall Bate was a thoroughly obscure anti-Separatist nonconforming minister who died while a prisoner in the Gatehouse on 2 October 1613. Cf. Burrage, *Early English Dissenters*, I:176; John Cotton, *Master John Cotton's Answer to Master Roger Williams*, ed. J. Lewis Diman, Publications of the Narragansett Club (Providence, 1867), II:192; *Romes Eccho or A Dialogue Betwixt a Papist and a Protestant* (n.p., 1641), sig. B2 (this tract is Wing STC R1899). Bate defended absolute congregational autonomy while insisting that a true particular church could remain pure although subject to Antichristian government: "What duties cannot be performed in publique, ought to be performed in private." Randal Bate, *Certain Observations of that Reverend, Religious and Faithful Servant of God, . . . Mr. Randal Bate* (Amsterdam, 1624?), pp. 26, 103, 148-49, 175-77 (the quoted passage), 185-92. His views on the latter point would presumably make him congenial to Leighton, who, in turn, in *Speculum Belli Sacri* (p. 115) refers to that persecuted "holy Father M.R.B.," suggesting that Leighton may have given Staresmore the manuscript of Bate's eleven year old tract. For Leighton's own anti-Separatist arguments see ibid., pp. 234-35.

38. Bradford, *History of Plymouth Plantation*, I:92. On 13 August 1618 John Chamberlain wrote Dudley Carleton that "There were likewise certain Brownists fined and imprisoned for following of conventicles." John Chamberlain, *The Letters of John Chamberlain*, ed. Norman E. McClure, 2 vols. (Philadelphia, 1939), II:165.

39. Leighton, *An Epitome*, pp. 67-68 (I have changed the original "Condomarian," a typographical error, to "Gondomarian"); SP 16/534, fol. 153v. (for this document see below, n.13, chap 4).

40. Johnson, "Exiled English Church," p. 239 identifies the author of the anonymous tract.

41. Leighton, *An Epitome*, pp. 4, 67. On the first news of Leighton's arrest the Rev. Joseph Meade identified him as follows: "This is he that some years since published a book called the Holy warre, and hath now lately printed another book called Sions plea. . . ." Meade to Sir Martin Stuteville, 27 February 1630, Harleian MS 390, fol. 498v. The version of this letter reprinted in Thomas Birch, comp., *The Court and Times of Charles I*, ed. R. F. Williams, 2 vols. (London, 1848), II:61 badly garbles this passage.

42. For the demand for military literature see Maurice J. D. Cockle, *A Bibliography of English Military Books up to 1642* (London, 1900). Leighton admits his amateur standing in technical matters at several points: *Speculum Belli Sacri*, pp. 32, 50, 167-68. The work, in fact, is mainly homiletic and polemical and not, as Gardiner would have it (*History of England*, VII:144), an instance of Leighton's "cool presumption."

43. Leighton, *Speculum Belli Sacri*, pp. 204, 120-21, 194-95, 195-96. Leighton also called the English military ensigns "the badge of the beast"

because of their popish crosses and he denounced the English invocation of St. George in battle. Ibid., pp. 58-59.

44. For the genesis of the book see Leighton, *An Epitome*, pp. 1-2.

45. As Johnson points out, the STC has reversed the two editions. Though very similar in typography, the Staresmore edition (STC 15430) is less perfect and earlier than Stam's (STC 15429). Johnson, "Exiled English Church," p. 240; Johnson, "J. F. Stam," p. 185. Stam copied Staresmore's work so closely the two editions must have come out about the same time, but there is a third edition clearly of a later date (its title page alludes to Leighton's imprisonment): Wing STC L 1022, conjecturally assigned to an unknown Amsterdam press of the 1640s. Leighton claimed that *Sions Plea* "cost me triple, to hasten it to Parliament," presumably a reference to his simultaneously engaging both Staresmore and Stam (*An Epitome*, p. 2).

46. Leighton alludes to the drowning of the Elector Frederick's eldest son "just at that time when this worke was finishing" (Sions Plea, p. 340). The event occurred on 7/17 January 1629. On 4/14 March Leighton wrote his wife from Utrecht that "I hope the parliament hath the thing ere this." SP 16/138, fols. 90r.-v.

47. Leighton claimed at his trial and later in his *Epitome* (pp. 2, 9) that he had a hand, at most, in sending over two copies of the piece. However, his son Robert wrote to his parents of seeing copies in Edinburgh as early as 20 May 1629. SP 16/142, fol. 241. Calvin Bruen of Chester, whom the bishop of the diocese described in 1637 as "a silly, but very seditious fellow," had also in 1630 obtained a copy for his shop "as soone as Doctor Laytons Booke came forth." William Prynne, *A New Discovery of the Prelates Tyranny in their Late Prosecutions of Mr. W. Pryn, . . . Dr. John Bastwick . . . and Mr. H. Burton* (London, 1641), p. 219. See also Richardson, *Puritanism in North-West England*, pp. 182-83. One copy, at least, did end up with a member of parliament: Sir Simonds D'Ewes. Andrew G. Watson, *The Library of Sir Simonds D'Ewes* (London, 1966), p. 182. Attorney General Sir Robert Heath called Leighton a liar, "for in his answer he denys he scattered any of thes books, and yet upon his examination he confesseth he dispersed divers of them." Samuel Rawson Gardiner, ed., *Speech of Sir R. Heath . . . in the Case of A. Leighton in the Star Chamber*, Camden Society, n. s., XIV (London, 1875):2.

48. Leighton, *Sions Plea*, p. 340.

49. Pride of place in emphasizing millenial expectations in English Protestant thought belongs, of course, to William Haller's *Foxe's Book of Martyrs and the Elect Nation* (London, 1963). It is, however, William Lamont and his critics who have set the terms of the current debate. Cf. William Lamont, *Godly Rule, Politics and Religion, 1603-60* (London, 1969) and the criticisms by Bernard Capp and Carol Z. Wiener. Bernard Capp, "The Millenium and Eschatology in England," *Past and Present*, LVII (1972):156-62, summarizes the author's exchanges with Lamont. A bibliography is provided in n.1 of Capp. Carol Z. Wiener, "The Beleaguered Isle. A Study of Elizabethan and Early Jacobean Anti-Catholicism," *Past and Present*, LI (1971):27-62.

50. Leighton, *Sions Plea*, pp. 235-40 (Amos is cited at p. 238), 274, 297ff.

The pervasive sense of crisis in English millenialism is well brought out in Wiener, "The Beleaguered Isle," a study whose importance is too easily obscured by its author's unfortunate and anachronistic allusions to American anti-Communism.

51. Leighton attacks Separatism in *Sions Plea*, pp. 84-86. Such was his pride in his ability to refute the Separatists by his distinction between the true churches and the Antichristian hierarchy imposed on them that John Canne complained of "this mans insolent boasting against us, and the untrue reports, which he giveth forth of refuting the *chiefest* separatists." John Canne, *A Necessitie of Separation From the Church of England* . . . (Amsterdam, 1634), pp. 154-55. For all the recent work on millenarianism, Antichrist first received his due as *the* enemy, not just one figure in the complicated scenario laid down in Revelations, in Christopher Hill, *Antichrist in Seventeenth-Century England* (London, 1971).

52. Leighton, *Sions Plea*, p. 151.

53. Ibid., pp. 157, 110, 234, 58ff. (the allegation that Bancroft organized the Gunpowder Plot can be found on pp. 76-77).

54. Ibid., pp. 139ff., 240. Leighton argues that submission to prelatical censures amounts to passive endorsement of the prelacy on pp. 31, 46-50.

55. Ibid., pp. 178, 171-72, 160-62, 176. "The daughter of Heth" is taken from Genesis 26: 34-35.

Notes to Chapter III

1. Brooke to Laud, 15 December 1630, SP 16/177, fol. 13r.

2. Leighton, *An Epitome*, p. 3; Gardiner, *History of England*, VII: 144-48; for Leighton at Utrecht see Raymond P. Stearns, *Congregationalism in the Dutch Netherlands: The Rise and Fall of the English Congregational Classis, 1621-1635* (Chicago, 1940), p. 91.

3. John Rushworth, *Historical Collections of Private Passages of State, Weighty Matters in Law, Remarkable Proceedings* . . ., 8 vols. (London, 1721-22), II:56.

4. In the original draft of his speech Heath left out the twelfth and thirteenth charges against Leighton, though in his final version he held the twelfth charge tantamount to an accusation of treason. Cf. SP 16/168, fol. 41r. (the original draft) with Gardiner, *Speech of Sir Robert Heath*, pp.7-8. The information can be found in the Inner Temple, Misc. MS no. 19, fols. 38-41. The material presented by Rushworth, *Historical Collections*, II:55-58, is not a reprint of the information but some sort of abstract or summary.

5. Leighton, *Sions Plea*, pp. 163-68; Leighton, *An Epitome*, pp. 19-20, 24-25. Leighton reprinted the full version of his answer in his *Epitome;* he actually submitted an abridged version (see ibid., p. 16), which is slightly milder than the full one but substantially the same in its argument. There are two extant copies of the abridged answer: at Inner Temple, Misc. MS no. 19, fols. 41-45, and British Library, Sloane MS 41.

6. "The City Censures concerning Leightons escape," SP 16/175, fol. 178r.

7. Joseph Meade reported the appearance of "The Devill and the Duke, for which on wednesday was much inquisition in Paules Church yard [i.e., among the booksellers there]" in a letter to Stuteville on 11 November 1626, Harleian MS 389, fol. 157r. (reprinted in Birch, *Court and Times*, I:169). In the next three years Meade recorded eight other libels or squibs against Buckingham as well as one instance in 1627 when the Earl of Lincoln's servants were apprehended posting papers against the forced loan. *Ibid.*, fols. 182r., 189r., 192r., 198v., 244v., 249, 314; Harleian MS 390, fols. 415r., 427. The Overbury story was part of a libel circulated by John Bastwick's brother-in-law in 1634 (see below, n. 3, chap. 5). While in the Netherlands in 1629 the elder Sir Henry Vane observed, "there is come to my hands a Scandalous and wicked libell, under the titles of Tom-tell-Truth and the practise of Princes: the one casting great imputations upon the person and government of King James of blessed memorie. The other, upon the King our Master and his present government; all tending to sedition." Vane to Dorchester, 16/26 December 1629, SP 84/140, fol. 199r. Dorchester brought the matter to the attention of Charles I himself. Dorchester to Vane, 6/16 January 1630, SP 84/141 fol. 10r. Similarly, the previous year the press of the Ancient Church turned out *The Spy* (STC 20577), a verse satire which attacked "Arminian" psuedopopery and Spanish treachery in violent terms as well as repeated the story that Buckingham poisoned James I with the aid of Dr. John Lambe. *The Spy* also attracted considerable government attention. Johnson, "Exiled English Church," p. 240; Greg, *Companion to Arber*, p. 248.

8. From the first draft of Heath's speech, SP 16/168, fol. 38r.

9. For Felton's behavior after his arrest see Birch, *Court and Times*, I:403-04, 413, 427, 438, 442, 445-46, 449-50.

10. Meade to Stuteville, 11 October 1628, Harleian MS 390, fol. 442v. (reprinted in Birch, *Court and Times*, I:410 with minor inaccuracies). Laud's views were similar (cf. his *Works*, I:83).

11. White, *Treatise of the Sabbath-Day*, sig. ***3r. Leighton is merely taken as the frankest representative of the "Presbyterian backbiters" (sig. ***r.), who include Cartwright, Travers, Udall, Penry, Martin Marprelate, Field, Wilcox, and the authors of the *Lincolnshire Abridgement*.

12. Laud to Wentworth, 26 April 1637, Laud, *Works*, VII: 342.

13. Laud, *Works*, III:207-10. See also Trevor-Roper, *Laud*, pp. 85-89, 93-94; Kenneth W. Shipps, "The Political Puritan," *Church History*, XLV (1976):200-02. Laud had a right to be nervous given the fate of his patron, but he did seem to take a rather morbid delight in chronicling every threat against his life. Cf. Laud, *Works*, III:220, VII:371-72, 373.

14. Laud labelled the paper "a threateninge Letter without name for the Imprisonment of D Leighton about Sions Plea." SP 16/161, fols. 80, 81. Cf. Heylyn, *Cyprianus Anglicus*, p. 198. Heylyn, however, conflates the threatening letter of 29 March 1629 with that (involving Leighton) of 20 February 1630. For Laud's belief that more than one man composed *Sions Plea* see Leighton, *An Epitome*, p. 68.

15. Meade to Stuteville, 27 February 1630, 27 November 1630, reprinted in Birch, *Court and Times*, II:61, 79-80. Cf. Leighton, *An Epitome*, pp. 3-4.

16. Cf. Leighton, *An Epitome*, pp. 18-19; Sloane MS 41, fol. 6r. For the relationship between these two versions of Leighton's answer see above, n. 5.

17. Gardiner, *Speech of Sir Robert Heath*, p. 3.

18. For Leighton's escape cf. Gardiner, *History of England*, VII: 151; Meade to Stuteville, 27 November 1630, Birch, *Court and Times*, II: 80. Meade implies here and on 5 December 1630 (ibid., II:83) that the escape involved considerably more premeditation than Gardiner will allow of. Of the event itself, Meade reported that Leighton's supporters claimed "he was delivered out of the prison by the prayer [of] the Church," but that others in London said "this flight of his had given a great blow to the cause by deserting it, which he should have stood more stoutly to. But alas he durst not for his eares." Harleian MS 390, fols. 522r.-v. (reprinted in Birch, *Court and Times*, II:80). The "City Censures" makes a similar point: the "Puritan generally" (that is, in general) regretted the escape because "they would not have had him have *disgraced* the truth by flying." SP 16/175, fol. 178r.

19. Meade to Stuteville, 5 December 1630, Harleian MS 390, fol. 525v. (reprinted in Birch, *Court and Times*, II:83).

20. Leighton, An Epitome, pp. 12-15, 90.

21. Gardiner, *Speech of Sir Robert Heath*, p. 10. In 1608 Richard Maunsell after taking the Star Chamber oath declined to name either the individuals who had given him printed copies of Nicholas Fuller's *Argument (The Argument of Master Nicholas Fuller in the Case of Thomas Lad and Richard Maunsell, his Clients* [The Netherlands?, 1607]) or the individuals to whom he passed them on and requested not to be "pressed" on the point because he would not bring "many others" into question (precisely Leighton's grounds for an identical refusal twenty-two years later). PRO, STAC 8/19/7, fols 1-2. Cf. Curtis, "William Jones," pp. 58-60. For Pickering's Case see below, p. 38.

22. Inner Temple MS no. 19, fol. 38v.

23. Leighton, *Sions Plea*, p. 158. Gardiner, *Speech of Sir Robert Heath*, pp. 3-4. Leighton held the power of parliament sufficient to abolish episcopacy despite the king's explicit command to the contrary, just as Absalom might be killed "notwithstanding of Davids command, out of his state-indangering indulgencie [,] to the contrarie." Leighton, *Sions Plea*, p. 175.

24. The quotation comes from Laud's annotation of Leighton's letter to his wife on 14 March 1629, in which he wrote her that "I hope the Parliament hath the thing ere this, I hope Mr. Pety would comfort you, who promised to have [?] a protection for me at my house against my overcoming." SP 16/138, fols. 90r.-v. This Maximillian Petty is probably the brother-in-law of Sir James Ley (who had some patronage at Westbury) and, presumptively, the uncle of Maximillian Petty the Leveller. Cf. Robert E. Ruigh, *The Parliament of 1624: Politics and Foreign Policy* (Cambridge, Mass., 1971), p. 53n.; G.D. Squibb, ed., *Wiltshire Visitation*

Pedigrees, 1623, Publications of the Harleian Society, CV-CVI (London, 1954):113; Anthony à Wood, *The Life and Times of Anthony Wood, Antiquary, at Oxford, 1632-95, as Described by Himself*, ed. Andrew Clark, 5 vols. (Oxford: 1891-1900), I:33, 33n., 35; G. E. Aylmer, "Gentlemen Levellers?," *Past and Present*, IL (1970):120.

As a matter of fact Westbury, Wiltshire *was* a likely place for a patron of Alexander Leighton to come from. Despite the Ley influence the borough elected the oppostion leader Sir Miles Fleetwood to the parliament of 1621, and in 1640 it twice returned the militant Puritan John Ashe, who had been indicted three years earlier for distributing *Newes from Ipswich* and *A Divine Tragedy*. See Mary F. Keeler, *The Long Parliament, 1640-41: A Biographical Study of its Members* (Philadelphia, 1954), pp. 91-92, 178-79.

25. The quotation comes from Meade's letter to Stuteville of 27 February 1630, written just after the arrest of Leighton and conveying only the popular report of the contents of *Sions Plea*. Harleian MS 390, fol. 498v. (badly garbled in Birch, *Court and Times*, II:61).

26. A significant portion of the entries in *Acts of the Privy Council* for the years 1629 and 1630 relates to rioting. For the East Anglian disturbances see John Walter and Keith Wrightson, "Dearth and the Social Order in Early Modern England," *Past and Present*, LXXI (1976):35-38; for the Western Risings cf. D. C. Allen, "The Risings in the West, 1628-31," *Economic History Review*, 2d ser., VI (1952):76-85; Eric Kerridge, "The Revolts in Wiltshire against Charles I," *Wiltshire Archaeological Magazine*, LVII (1958-59):64-75. The mobbing of Lambe and the execution of Felton are described in Gardiner, *History of England*, VI:319-20, 353-56; Birch, *Court and Times*, I:442.

27. One does not have to accept all of Christopher Hill's arguments on the social structure of Stuart England to appreciate his account of contemporary notions of "popular" attributes in "The Many-Headed Monster in Late Tudor and Early Stuart Political Thinking," *From the Renaissance to the Counter Reformation: Essays in Honour of Garrett Mattingly*, ed. Charles H. Carter (New York, 1965), pp. 296-324. The institutional thought of Caroline administrators (excepting Strafford and Laud) is not the most studied of topics, but there is a rather persuasive essay on the general subject by Michael Hawkins, "The Government: Its Role and Its Aims," in *The Origins of the English Civil War*, ed. Conrad Russell (London, 1973), pp. 35-65.

28. Bodleian Library, Douce MS 173, fol. 9r. See also Conrad Russell, "The Theory of Treason in the Trial of Strafford," *English Historical Review*, LXXX (1965):31-33.

29. The other three cases were those of Sir John Eliot et al., Richard Chambers, and the Earls of Bedford and Clare et al. (the first of these was ultimately tried in the Court of Kings Bench, but it began as an action in the Star Chamber).

30. "The City Censures," SP 16/175, fol. 178r. Even Joseph Meade, no admirer of Laud or Laudians complained of "the jealousies and rash censures of the people" in mindlessly condemning John Cosin's book of private devotions. Meade to Stuteville, 18 May 1627, Harleian MS 390, fol.

25lv. (reprinted under an odd heading in Birch, *Court and Times*, I:227).

31. Samuel Rawson Gardiner, ed., *Documents Relating to the Proceedings Against W. Prynne, in 1634 and 1637*, Camden Society n. s., XVIII (London, 1877):19, 27.

32. Peter Heylyn, *A Brief and Moderate Answer to the Seditious and Scandalous Challenge of H. Burton* (London, 1637), pp. 188-89.

33. Leighton, *Sions Plea*, pp. 337ff. Gardiner, of course, noticed the passage: *History of England*, VII, 146.

34. Gardiner, *Speech of Sir Robert Heath*, pp. 7-8; Leighton, *Sions Plea*, p. 208.

35. Pickering's Case, or De Libellis Famosis, became the precedent for future libel prosecutions because of the scope of the judgment rendered by Star Chamber in 1605. It is recorded in John Hawarde's *Les Reportes del Cases in Camera Stellata, 1593 to 1609*, ed. William P. Baildon (n.p., 1894), pp. 222-30, and briefed in Sir Edward Coke, *The Fift[h] Part of the Reports of Sir Edward Coke, Kt.* (London, 1605), pp. 125-26. Cf. also *The Twelfth Part of the Reports of Sir Edward Coke, Kt.* (London, 1656), pp. 132-34, and for Pickering's role in the Puritans' maneuverings in 1603 see Collinson, *Elizabethan Puritan Movement*, pp. 450, 452.

36. For Dorset's remarks see below, p. 42; for Laud, *Works*, VII: 317 (Laud to Wentworth, 11 February 1637).

Notes to Chapter IV

1. See Greg, *Companion to Arber*, pp. 242-50 and n. 12, chap. 5 below. Meade mentions that Prynne's attacks on Montague got him into trouble with the High Commission as early as 30 November 1627. Harleian MS 390, fol. 327r. (not reprinted in Birch, *Court and Times*). For Prynne's attitude towards episcopacy prior to 1633 see William Lamont, *Marginal Prynne, 1600-1669* (London, 1963), pp. 11-27.

2. Gardiner, *Documents*, p. 14; Greg, *Companion to Arber*, pp. 279-82.

3. For Brewer's conventicles see n. 7, chap. 2 above; Laud, *Works*, V:347. For Leighton n. 47, chap. 5 below; for Bastwick, pp. 48-49 below.

4. Gardiner, *Documents*, pp. 12-13. For an account of the trial see Lamont, *Marginal Prynne*, pp. 30-33.

5. For Prynne's distinctly humble defense see Gardiner, *Documents*, pp. 14-15. Prynne's threatening letter to Laud of 11 June 1634 is reprinted in ibid., pp. 32-57. His earlier petitions for pardon are reprinted in Greg, *Companion to Arber*, pp. 283-84, 289.

6. For Laud's speech at the trial see above, p. 12. The version given in Gardiner, *Documents*, p. 27, differs slightly in wording but not in substance.

7. For Prynne's use of this defense see his letter to Laud, 11 June 1634, ibid., pp. 43ff.

8. Rushworth, *Historical Collections*, II:232.

9. Heath's words as given in Bodleian Library, Douce MS 173, fols. 8r.-v. are: "Libells are the most part short; cominge immediately from the breast, But this is soe long that it hath made a Large Volumen." Cf. his remarks quoted above, p. 000; Vane's remark comes from Gardiner, *Documents*, p. 23; Dorset's from Rushworth, *Historical Collections*, II:241.

10. Heylyn began collecting seditious extracts from Prynne's works as early as May 1628. See the testimony of John Eaton before the Long Parliament, Simonds D'Ewes, *The Journal of Sir Simonds D'Ewes From the Beginning of the Long Parliament to the Opening of the Trial of the Earl of Stratford*, ed. Wallace Notestein (New Haven, 1923), p. 158.

11. Heath's comments are in Gardiner, *Documents*, p. 18; Juxon's in ibid., p. 24; Dorset's in Rushworth, *Historical Collections*, II:238.

12. According to Prynne, Laud suggested frequently both in private and in the Star Chamber "*that my Histriomastix was compiled by combinacion . . . it being impossible for any man of what profession soever, though sixty years old to peruse or read all those authorities quoted in it.*" Gardiner, *Documents*, pp. 34-35. Three years earlier Laud had similarly claimed that Leighton did not have the learning to compile *Sions Plea*, "for all the *rare wits* (saith he of the Land for *Law and Divinity*) have been at the making of it." Leighton, *An Epitome*, p. 68.

13. SP 16/534, fols. 153v., 154v. The paper in question is unsigned but its form is identical to that described by Heylyn himself and examined by D'Ewes during Heylyn's own interrogation by the Long Parliament. Heylyn, *Cyprianus Anglicus*, p. 230; D'Ewes, *Journal*, pp. 132, 186-87.

14. The proceedings of Prynne's trial taken from British Library, Add. MSS, 11, 764 and reprinted (with minor errors) in Camden Society, n. s., XVIII, do not mention Leighton at all nor does the account in Bodleian Library, Douce MS 173. However, the version of the trial in Rushworth, *Historical Collections*, II:220 dated 7 February 1634 gives Leighton a prominent place as does the copy of the original Star Chamber information (dated 29 July 1633) seen by D'Ewes during the Long Parliament's investigation of Prynne's case. D'Ewes, *Journal*, p. 130. On the question of Heylyn's objection to Prynne's translation of Bodine cf. SP 16/534, fol. 149r; Gardiner, *Documents*, p. 7.

15. Rushworth, *Historical Collections*, II:222-23.

16. William Prynne, *Histriomastix. The Players Scourge* (London, 1633), pp. 488, 698. Prynne never cites *Sions Plea* but only *Speculum Belli Sacri* and the anonymous *Short Treatise* against stage players. For the contrast between Leighton and Prynne see Lamont, *Marginal Prynne*, pp. 45-46.

17. For Sherfield's case see T. B. Howell, ed., *Cobbett's Complete Collection of State Trials and Proceedings for High Treason and Other Crimes and Misdemeanours From the Earliest Period to the Present Time*, 33 vols. (London, 1809-28), III:519-61; Trevor-Roper, *Laud*, pp. 110-11.

18. Gardiner, *Documents*, p. 18; Rushworth, *Historical Collections*, II:234-35.

19. Rushworth, *Historical Collections*, II:236.

20. Bodleian Library, Douce MS 173, fol. 3r. Edmund Peacham in 1615 and a barrister named Williams in 1619 were convicted of treason in just such circumstances. Howell, *State Trials*, II:870-79, 1086-87.

21. Rushworth, *Historical Collections*, II:237.

22. Gardiner, *Documents*, p. 23. The words are those of Sir Thomas Edmonds, who had been one of the moderates in Sherfield's case.

23. Laud, *Works*, VI:42. "Some of them" apparently refers to Henry Burton.

24. William Prynne, *The Unbishoping of Timothy and Titus* (Amsterdam, 1636), pp. 147ff.

25. Lamont argues (*Marginal Prynne*, pp. 41-67) that Prynne did not become a true radical until 1641, a difficult proposition to establish because after 1637 Prynne was unable to publish anything until his release by the Long Parliament. But the earliest edition of *A Catalogue of Such Testimonies in all Ages as Plainly Evidence Bishops and Presbyters to Be One, Equall and the Same Jurisdiction* (Holland, 1637), p. 18, already takes this hard line on episcopacy. To be sure, Prynne holds only "Lordly Prelacy" (episcopacy defended by *jure divino* claims) to be downright popish and Antichristian (ibid., p. 10), but he nevertheless is urging the total abolition of episcopacy, not a return to some Elizabethan ideal, although he does not claim that some other form of polity is the true *jure divino* one. *A Catalogue* is clearly a Dutch product: the type face, initial letters, and ornaments (especially the title page headpiece, the turned chain line on p. 3, and the small initial "T") are identical to John Bastwick's *Letany*. For the printers of the latter work see below, n. 8, chap. 5. It would, however, be incautious to attribute the work to any given Dutch printer purely on the basis of typography.

26. Michael Sparke, *A Catalogue of Printed Books Written by W. Prynne . . .* (London, 1643), p. 3; William Prynne, *The Antipathie of the English Prelacie, Both to Regall Monarchy, and Civil Unity* (London, 1641), Epistle Dedicatory. For the significance of this work see Lamont, *Marginal Prynne*, pp. 67-83. Lamont suggests, pp. 81-83, that Prynne borrowed heavily from *Sions Plea* for *The Antipathie*, a possibility but, again, a difficult proposition to establish on purely internal evidence. An expanded version of *A Catalogue*, probably also published in 1641 (British Library copy 108.c.8), does invoke *Sions Plea* in the new preface, sig.ar., and asserts, sig. av., "why the churches of Scotland, and *England* may not now be governed by Presbyters only without Bishops, as well as at first [i.e., as in the primitive church], I cannot conceive." There is, however, no other hard evidence of a link, personal or intellectual, between the two men.

27. Prynne, *The Unbishoping*, pp. 5, 10 (and margin), 117, 118, 159-60.

Notes to Chapter V

1. For Bastwick's relation to Leighton see above, pp. 15-16. Bastwick mentions his "long acqueyntance" with Prynne and Henry Burton in his answer to the Star Chamber indictment of 1637. John Bastwick, *The Answer of John Bastwick . . . to the Information of Sir John Bancks* (Leyden, 1637). p. 5 (STC 1568).

2. In 1645 a former neighbor of Bastwick's recalled that while in Colchester he "did much good among the people" until "the Prelate of *Canterbury* by his Purseuvants fetcht him from thence," but again no details are given. B. S., *Innocency Cleared . . . in a Letter Sent to Mr. H. Burton . . . in Defence of Dr. Bastwick* (London, 1645), p. 6. For the trial itself, see below, n. 4.

3. William Lynne to Laud, 29 October 1634, SP 16/276, fol. 124r. Cotton's activities included spreading pamphlets about the alleged poisonings of Prince Henry and King James. William Lynne to Secretary Sir Francis Windebank, 7 January 1635, SP 16/282, fol. 46r.

4. The fullest account of the charges against Bastwick and the manner of deciding them can be found at SP 16/261, fols. 178v.-179r. D'Ewes (*Journal*, p. 232) notes that the charges were originally brought by "Mr. Newcomin of Colchester and others who had combined and complotted together to accuse him"; presumably, then, the High Commission did not initiate the proceedings.

5. Mary Hume Maguire, "Attack of the Common Lawyers on the Oath Ex Officio as Administered in the Ecclesiastical Courts in England," in *Essays in History and Political Theory in Honor of Charles Howard McIlwain* (Cambridge, Mass., 1936), pp. 213ff.; Ronald A. Marchant, *The Church Under Law: Justice, Administration and Discipline in the Diocese of York, 1560-1640* (London, 1969), p. 4; Roland G. Usher, *The Rise and Fall of the High Commission* (Oxford, 1913), pp. 265-67.

6. SP 16/261, fols. 97r.-v; Usher, *Rise and Fall*, pp. 325-27.

7. John Bastwick, *A Just Defence of John Bastwick Against the Calumnis of John Lilburne* (London, 1645), pp. 37ff. In one version of his speech at his trial in 1637 Bastwick says the *Apologeticus* was printed "beyond seas" and in another that "I sent my Book over [to England?] by a Dutch Merchant." Prynne, *New Discovery*, p. 19 (2d pag.); John Bastwick, *A Briefe Relation of Certain Speciall and Most Materiall . . . Passages, and Speeches in the Starre-Chamber . . . at the Censure of . . . Dr. Bastwicke, Mr. Burton and Mr. Prynne* (Amsterdam, 1638), p. 11 (STC 1570).

8. John Lilburne, *The Christian Mans Triall: Or a True Relation of the First Apprehension and Severall Examinations of John Lilburne* (London, 1641), pp. 2-4, 22; see also Pauline Gregg, *Free-Born John: A Biography of John Lilburne* (London, 1961), pp. 27-29. For James Moxon see Joseph Moxon, *Mechanick Exercises on the Whole Art of Printing, 1683-4*, ed. Herbert Davis and Harry Carter, 2d ed. (London, 1962), pp. xix-xxi. Johnson, "Willem Christiaans," pp. 121-23, incorrectly assigns all four parts of the Letany (STC 1572-75) to that printer and his Leyden press on

the basis of typographical evidence, but Christiaans admitted printing only Bastwick's *Answer* to the Star Chamber information (STC 1568). See SP 84/153,fol. 271r.; SP 84/154, fol. 150r. (both documents deal with Christiaans's punishment on 3/13 April 1638 for printing books insulting to the English authorities). Moreover, the English stationer Matthew Symonds when interrogated about his trip to the Netherlands testified that "at my coming there Dr. Basticke[s] thinges were then in the presse printed by one James Moxon." The manuscript was supplied by "one Mr. John, and when the 5 [*sic*] partes were all done then the saide Mr. John shipped away of each part of quantitie, I think 1000 of each." SP 16/387, fol. 148r. (dated 14 April 1638). Even the typography of the *Letany* is consistent with Moxon's known work, especially STC 13265, his edition of Henry Hexham, *A True and Brief Relation of the Famous Siege of Breda* (Delft, 1637).

9. Matthew Brookes to Bishop Matthew Wren, 27 November 1637, Bodleian Library, Tanner MS 68, fol. 283v. ("barm" means "yeasty" or "heady"). Cf. Clement Corbett to Wren, 17 November 1637, 21 November 1637, ibid., fols. 9v., 10r. For Burroughs's entire career see Kenneth W. Shipps, "Lay Patronage of East Anglian Puritan Clerics in Pre-Revolutionary England (Ph.D. diss., Yale University, 1971), pp. 163-64, 240. I am indebted to Professor Shipps for bringing this account of the smuggling of the *Letany* to my attention.

10. In addition to the material mentioned in notes 7, chap. 3, and 3 above, some perspective on the *Letany* can be acquired from considering that between October 1631 and June 1632 the High Commission handled among other matters the case of a minister who added a scandalous table to the Psalms, an accusation against Michael Sparke, the bookseller, for similarly interpolating a "scurvy letter" against Cambridge University in his edition of the Psalms, the famous instance of the King's Printer producing a Bible with blasphemous "misprints" so obvious they can only have been deliberate, the case of another bookseller who brought out a book with abusive passages against Queen Elizabeth, and that of still another bookseller who issued a blasphemous series of biblical ballads and who defended himself by testifying "that the same was printed before he was borne, and he hath but renewed it." For its part the Star Chamber in roughly the same period also handled several libels, the most interesting being the case of five defendants who allegedly charged their neighbors with adultery by composing and circulating "a scandalous lybell in meter or verses . . . ending with a scurrilous verse, wench lye still, and c . . . " Gardiner, *Cases in the Courts of Star Chamber and High Commission*, pp. 149, 268, 296, 305, 314.

11. Bastwick, *Answer*, p. 5; Prynne, *New Discovery*, pp. 18-19 (2d pag.).

12. For Burton's connections with Bastwick see above, notes 1 and 3. Burton cites Bastwick's case in the High Commission several times as instances of episcopal tyranny. Henry Burton, *For God, and the King. The Summe of Two Sermons Preached on the Fifth of November . . . 1636* (Amsterdam, 1636), pp. 67-70, 122, 153. Lamont (*Marginal Prynne*, pp. 33-35) stresses the lack of affinity between Burton and Prynne. Without taking issue with this point, it is also worth remembering that the common

targets and tactics of the two men led to their being regularly linked together in the period 1627-30. Thus, Meade to Stuteville on 15 November 1628: "Mr. Burton, Mr. Prinne of Lyncolnes Inne and some others having bin long in the High Commission for printing of unlicensed books against Arminianisme, Mr. Prynne of Friday was senight even when he was ready for sentence presented my Lord of London with a prohibition from the Judges of the Common Pleas obteined the day before . . . " Laud allegedly uttered angry threats against any other defendant who would bring in a prohibition, and the next to do so, predictably, was Burton. Harleian MS 390, fol. 455r. (not reprinted in Birch, *Court and Times*); Henry Burton, *A Narration of the Life of Mr. Henry Burton* (London, 1643), pp. 4-5. See also Benjamin Laney to John Cosin, 25 June 1629, in Birch, *Court and Times*, II:19.

13. Burton, *A Narration*, pp. 4-5; Birch, *Court and Times*, I:227, 229.

14. Henry Burton, *Israels Fast. Or, a Meditation Upon the Seventh Chapter of Joshuah* (London, 1628), "The Epistle," sig. A3v. This edition is STC 4146, the "Rochel" imprint STC 4147.

15. Burton, *A Narration*, p. 5. The High Commission, however, was apparently oblivious to the preface to the sermon, sigs. Bv.-B3v., which uses the heading "Neutralizers" to cover such "Achans" as Cosin, Montague, Mainwaring, and, by way of a punning verse, Laud. The parallels with Buckingham are most evident on pp. 34-37.

16. Leighton, *Sions Plea*, p. 331; White, *A Treatise of the Sabbath-Day*, sig. **2r (margin); Heylyn, *Brief and Moderate Answer*, p. 88. For Burton's quarrel with White see the former's *A Plea to an Appeale: Traversed Dialogue Wise* (London, 1626), sig. avr. "Presbyterian backbiters" is White's phrase; "furious Aerian heretics" comes from Laud, *Works*, VI:574.

17. Burton, *A Narration*, p. 8.

18. SP 16/335, fols. 131-41 (the quotations are at fols. 133r., 135r. respectively).

19. Burton, *A Narration*, pp. 10-11; Burton, *For God and the King*, p. 8.

20. The original information, now badly damaged, along with a nineteenth century transcription may be found in SP 16/354, while there is another contemporary copy (dated 11 March 1637) in British Library, Add. MSS, 11, 308.

21. Contemporary speculation over the authorship is discussed in Lamont, *Marginal Prynne*, pp. 37-38. My evidence for the attributions of author and printer made in this paragraph is supplied in the appendix.

22. Johnson, "J. F. Stam," p. 186.

23. Burrage, *Early English Dissenters*, I:182, puts Staresmore in a London prison in 1635, apparently on the basis of an entry in *Calendar of State Papers Domestic, Charles I, 1635-36*, p. 88. Actually, the High Commission records (SP 16/261, fol. 266v.) are ambiguous at this point, and the "Sabrine" or "Sabrina" Staresmore referred to may be a woman and not the printer at all, but he does drop from sight in Amsterdam about this time.

24. Johnson attributes these second editions to an unknown London press, but for the case against this theory see the appendix where the evidence in favor of Canne will also be discussed.

25. See below, p. 76.

26. Edward Rossingham to Sir Thomas Puckering, 7 February 1637, Birch, *Court and Times*, II:274.

27. For Boye's unorthodox ideas about "absolute" prayers, for his Separatism, and for his West Country connections see his *The Importunate Beggar for Things Necessary* (Amsterdam, 1635), sig. B4r.; *A Just Defence of the Importunate Beggars Importunity* (n.p., 1636), sig. C2r.; and, two attacks on Boye by Edward Norris, *A Treatise Maintaining that Temporall Blessings are to bee Sought and Asked with Submission to the Will of God* (London, 1636), *passim*, and *The New Gospel, not the True Gospel; or, a Discovery of . . . Mr. I. Traske* (London, 1638), pp. 30-35. The printer of *The Importunate Beggar* (which is STC 3450) is identified in Johnson, "J. F. Stam," p. 186, while the printer of *A Just Defence* (STC 3451) is not known. For Boye's connection with the Jacob-Southwark church and through it with Staresmore and Canne see Burrage, *Early English Dissenters*, I:321, II:299 (where the name is spelled "Boy"). Norris implies in *The New Gospel*, p. 4, that Boye shared the Antinomian views of the notorious John Traske, who finally joined the Jacob church a little before his death in 1636 (ibid., p. 8; Burrage, *Early English Dissenters*, II:300, where the name is spelled "Trash").

28. For Ashe see above, n. 24, chap. 3; Keeler, *The Long Parliament*, pp. 91-92; *Winthrop Papers*, III:400-01. He is the unnamed "clothier in the county of Gloucester [*sic*]" mentioned in Rossingham's letter, Birch, *Court and Times*, II:275, as "a very precise man, and full of zeal to have dispersed these books . . . " Ashe had also come into conflict with Laud over the communion table in a church at Beckington, where he was lord of the manor (Laud, *Works*, IV:123-24), so neither he nor Boye could be considered inconspicuous when they undertook to distribute clandestine literature.

29. The "foot post" is described by Sir William Boswell, SP 84/153, fols. 301r.-v.; Christiaans's activities come from the testimony of Matthew Symmons, SP 16/387, fol. 148r. See also Johnson, "Willem Christiaans," p. 122. Coleman Street had a considerable reputation as a home for Puritan militants of various persuasions. See Pearl, *London and the Outbreak of the Puritan Revolution*, pp. 183-84.

30. For Laud's attempt at "counter-propaganda" see Trevor-Roper, *Laud*, p. 324. The two books are Dow's *Innovations Unjustly Charged* and Heylyn's *Brief and Moderate Answer*.

31. Laud to Wentworth, 28 June 1637, *Works*, VII:355.

32. For accounts of the famous trial of the Triumvirate see Gardiner, *History of England*, VII:228-33; Trevor-Roper, *Laud*, pp. 319-22.

33. Laud's analysis of the tracts is in SP 16/354, fols. 357r.-359v.

34. In 1636 Prynne published with Stam *Certaine Quaeres Propounded to Bowers at the Name of Jesus* (STC 20456), *The Lords Day, the Sabbath Day. Or, a Briefe Answer to . . . a Late Treatise of the Sabbath-Day . . .* (STC 20468), and *The Unbishoping of Timothy and Titus*. He also brought out *A Looking-Glasse for all Lordly Prelates* with another press, which I have suggested (see the appendix) was probably also Dutch. For sheer violence of antiepiscopal sentiments the latter two works afford, if

anything, better grounds for indictment than *Newes from Ipswich* (n.p., 1636). In particular, *The Unbishoping*, pp. 140-44, rehearses the same anecdotes about Wren and his commissary Dade, exhorts suspended ministers to go on in their ministry (p. 147), and repeatedly threatens (pp. 22-34, 160, and *passim*) the bishops with the plague or similar judgment as divine retribution for their Antichristian deeds. The next year Prynne would write of episcopal officers that "Certainly, hanging is to good for them." William Prynne, *A Quench-Coale. Or, a Briefe . . . Inquirie in What Place . . . the Lords-Table Ought to be Situated* (Amsterdam, 1637), p. 21 (STC 20474).

35. Prynne, *New Discovery*, pp. 8-9 (2d pag.), 152 (2d pag.).

36. The question of the printers was of more than abstract interest in the spring of 1637 while the Star Chamber was simultaneously engaged in drawing up a new edict to tighten regulation of the press. See below, pp. 63-64 and Gardiner, *History of England*, VIII:234.

37. For the abuse of *pro confesso* and *ore tenus* procedures in the Caroline Star Chamber see Henry E. I. Phillips, "The Last Years of the Court of Star Chamber, 1630-41," *Transactions of the Royal Historical Society*, 4th ser., XXI (1939):113-14. Under normal circumstances the greater use of written procedures (with due time for consultation with counsel) made the Star Chamber oath acceptable to men who rejected the legality of the High Commission's oath *ex officio*. See Nathaniel Wickens, *Wood Street-Compters Plea for its Prisoner* (Amsterdam, 1638), p. 30 (STC 25587). "Nathaniel Wickens," the name of Prynne's servant, is probably a pseudoym for Prynne himself. Cf. William Prynne, *The Lyar Confounded: Or, a Briefe Refutation of John Lilburne's . . . Case* (London, 1645), p. 26.

38. Prynne, *New Discovery*, p. 187; Leighton, *An Epitome*, p. 29; D'Ewes, *Journal*, p. 424.

39. William Hudson, *A Treatise of the Star Chamber* in *Collectanea Juridica*, ed. Francis Hargrave, 2 vols. (London, 1791-92), II:126-27. For Hudson see the *Dictionary of National Biography*, s.v. "Hudson, William." His treatise was written between 1625 and 1634 and is of particular interest as the work of a man who served for the defense in Leighton's case and for the prosecution in Prynne's.

40. Hudson, *A Treatise*, pp. 126-27.

41. Ibid., pp. 161-62.

42. Cf. the actual sentencing of the Triumvirate (Howell, *State Trials*, III:717-25) with Hudson's idealized description of the moment of judgment (Hudson, *A Treatise*, pp. 21-22), which emphasizes the manifest fairness of the whole Star Chamber's public proceedings and its consequent effect once sentence is pronounced on the defendant: "the world and people that see him are much moved then to hatred of his offence, and terrified by his example of punishment, as it is pronounced, he there standing before their eyes . . . "

43. British Library, Add.MSS, 11, 308, fol. 97v. *Newes from Ipswich* received special attention as "a pernitious damnable scurrilous Invective, and libell tendinge to the Incytinge [of] the people to use their force and power in factious, and discontented wayes . . . " (fols. 101v.-102r.). For the

Ipswich riot see W. E. Layton, "Ecclesiastical Disturbances in Ipswich During the Reign of Charles I," *East Anglian*, n.s., II (1887-88): 209, 257, 315, 373, 405; Shipps, "Lay Patronage," pp. 267-99.

44. Laud, *Works*, VI:43, 44.

45. Prynne, *New Discovery*, pp. 33-66 (2d pag.). Cf. Henry Jacie to John Winthrop, Jr., 18 August 1637, *Winthrop* Papers, III:486-87.

46. See Gerrard to Conway, ca. July 1637, cited above, n. 1, chap. 2; Rossingham to ?, 13 July 1637, SP 16/363, fol. 219r. (reprinted in Gardiner, *Documents*, p. 91); and, for the beaver hat the testimony of James Ingram, 22 September 1637, SP 16/368, fol. 26r.

47. SP 16/408, fol. 319; Leighton, *An Epitome*, pp. 85-86. Leighton's visitors included a young Puritan cleric, Samuel Rogers, who recorded in his diary for 5 July 1638: "I visit Dr. Laiton in the fleet; a Scotch spi[ritually] right; but sure upright and one that hath tasted of other sweetnes of Christ, even in this affliction." MS Diary, Percy Collection, Queens University, Belfast, fol. 23v. My thanks to Professor Kenneth Shipps, who is preparing an edition of the diary, for providing me with a transcription of this passage.

48. John Lilburne, *A Worke of the Beast, Or a Relation of a Most Unchristian Censure, Executed Upon J. Lilburne* (Amsterdam, 1638), p. 26.

49. Dow, *Innovations Unjustly Charged*, p. 63.

Notes to Chapter VI

1. There is, in fact, no general account of this subject except for Rostenberg's *The Minority Press and the English Crown*, which pays little attention to distribution and circulation, as against printing, and concentrates mainly on Elizabethan Puritan printing, especially the Martin Marprelate episode. My own description is derived primarily from the Star Chamber testimony about the distribution of Nicholas Fuller's *Argument* in 1608, STAC 8/19/7, fols. 1-13 (which should be considered in conjunction with Mark Curtis's "William Jones"); the documents on the circulation of foreign books in 1630 reprinted in Greg, *Companion to Arber*, pp. 253-57; the information on the smuggling of William Ames's *Fresh Suit* in 1633 in ibid., pp. 290-91; on the smuggling of bibles and prayer books in 1634-35 in ibid., pp. 305-09; the information in SP 16 and elsewhere (which will be cited in the appropriate places) on the distribution of *A Divine Tragedy* and *Newes from Ipswich* in 1636-37; and, the testimony of Matthew Symmons in 1638 on his recent trip to the Netherlands, SP 16/387, fols. 147-48.

2. Thus Symmons's frequently quoted observation (SP 16/387, fol. 148r.): "The shipmasters have a way as they say to Cozen the devill that is if they have anie prohibited goodes in theyre ship, then they strik upon the

sandes at quinneborrow and send away all theyre passingers and deliver all these prohibited goodes in some small boate or hige [hoy] and then can com off the sandes without anie danger." Throughout his testimony Symmons emphasizes the role of English merchants trading with the Netherlands in bringing the books over.

3. On this point, at least, Michael Sparke and Archbishop Laud were in agreement. Sparke complained of the high price of English bibles and the consequent Dutch competition in *Scintilla, or A Light Broken into Darke Warehouses* (London, 1641), reprinted in Edward Arber, ed., *A Transcript of the Registers of the Company of Stationers of London, 1554-1640 A. D.*, 5 vols. (London and Birmingham, 1875-94), IV:36. Sparke knew whereof he spoke: he was apprehended dealing in smuggled books in 1631 (Greg, *Companion to Arber*, pp. 262-65). For the background of *Scintilla*, see Cyprian Blagden, *The Stationers' Company: A History, 1403-1959* (London, 1960), pp. 131-34. Oddly enough, Laud too complained in 1632 of the bad workmanship and high cost of bibles printed under the Barker Patent, and of the superior and cheaper products available from "Amsterdam." Gardiner, *Cases in the Courts of Star Chamber and High Commission*, pp. 296-97.

4. The figures for Moxon come from Symmons's testimony; for Christiaans and Stam see Johnson, "J. F. Stam," pp. 187-93; "Willem Christiaans," p. 123. Symmons (SP 16/387, fol. 147v.) puts Stam's production of duodecimo bibles alone at 7,000 in 1637 (given Stam's contract for 6,000 bibles in 1644, duly recorded in a notarial record, this estimate of 1637 would tend to confirm Symmons's accuracy in general). For notarial contracts for bibles involving both of the Dutch printers and one Thomas Crafforth see M. M. Kleerkooper, *De Boekhande te Amsterdam, Voornamelijk in de 17e Eeuw*, 2 vols. ('s-Gravenhage, 1914-16), II:1244-46, 1453-54.

5. For Bayly and his book see Trevor-Roper, *Laud*, p. 188; H. S. Bennett, *English Books and Readers, 1603-1640: Being a Study in the History of the Book Trade in the Reigns of James I and Charles I* (Cambridge, 1970), pp. 102-03. Symmons noted (SP 16/387, fol. 147v.) that a Dutch printer, "John Johnson of Amsterdam printeth practise of pieties by tenn-thousand at a time his vent is most by marchantes." The printer in question is rather better known under the name of Jan Janszon of the firm of Hondius and Blaeu, printers of Mercator's atlas.

6. Burrage, *Early English Dissenters*, II:272; Greg, *Companion to Arber*, p. 291. Staresmore's successor John Canne had no better luck: despite his publication of potentially popular devotional works by John Preston, Richard Sibbes, and Thomas Hooker, and later an important annotated bible, as late as 1647 he repeatedly denied that his press had ever shown a profit. See his letters to the merchant William Sykes (who paid for part of the operation), reprinted by Burrage in *Transactions of the Baptist Historical Society*, III (1912-13):225-33.

7. Sykes's subsidy for the Richt Right press and Brewer's for the Pilgrim press are cases in point, and Symmons in 1638 noted a patron for virtually every important product of the Dutch commercial presses: a mysterious

"Mr. John" paid for most of the Puritan works turned out by Moxon, while "a scotch gentlemen" named "Hage" paid for the tracts Christiaans did not choose to print for free.

8. Symmons described Christiaans (SP 16/387, fol. 147v.) as having already printed Lily's "rules" and "hath bargained for to print the grammer with the same man that did Liles rules . . ." This man in turn had also arranged for a pirated edition of Clement Cotton's popular concordance to the bible. Lily's works, at least, were very lucrative. See Greg, *Companion to Arber*, p. 204 and pp. 178-207 *passim*.

9. Greg, *Companion to Arber*, p. 308. Cf. Sir William Boswell's comment on "The negligence, or falsehood of the searchers" in 1633, ibid., p. 291; John Lilburne, *A Copy of a Letter written by J. Lilburne . . . to J. Ingram and H. Hopkins* (n.p., 1640?), p. 4 (the tract is STC 15597).

10. The distributors of Nicholas Fuller's *Argument* in 1608 and of an unnamed seditious work in 1630 followed this method of operation exactly. See Curtis, "William Jones," pp. 59-60; Greg, *Companion to* Arber, pp. 253-57. In both cases copies of the books in question were eventually turned over to the High Commission.

11. Thus, Sir William Boswell's complaint that he received tardy notice of scandalous books printed in Holland "because they are commonly sold only to such as are thought to like them." Boswell to Laud, 16/26 May 1639, SP 84/155, fol. 145r.

12. SP 16/346, fol. 132 (Penton's examination on 7 February 1637 and Chillington's letter of transmittal of 7 December 1636); SP 16/349, fols. 99r.-v. (Chillington's examination, 7 March 1637). Chillington, an apprentice buttonmaker, was to pay Boye 2d. per copy for *Newes from Ipswich* and 6d. for *A Divine Tragedy*, and receive 3d. and 8d. respectively from Penton. Star Chamber, however, apparently thought him more than just a young man out for easy money since he and his master George Kendall were both included in the Star Chamber information against Burton, Bastwick, and Prynne although Penton was left out despite his more sinister reputation and the crowd of "many women" who tried to free him when he was arrested. For Chillington's later career, see Bernard S. Capp, *The Fifth Monarchy Men; A Study in Seventeenth-Century English Millenarianism* (London, 1972), p. 245.

13. Lilburne, *The Christian Mans Triall*, 2d ed., pp. 7-10; Gregg, *Free-Born John*, pp. 54-55.

14. Some of Thomas Scott's pamphlets went through four editions, but always within a period of a year; none could sustain the continuing interest of the *Abridgment*, which in a concise, and, therefore, inexpensive and easily smuggled form laid out the broadest common denominators of English nonconformity. The work had three distinct editions (STC 15646-48) prior to the Civil War: 1605 (William Jones, Sr. and/or Richard Schilders), 1617 (the Pilgrim Press), and 1638 (Willem Christiaans). Its influence was sufficient to provoke one of the longest running of the Puritan-conformist exchanges. The Calvinist bishop, Thomas Morton, replied to the 1617 edition with *A Defense of the Innocencie of the Three Ceremonies of the Church of England* (London, 1618) (STC 18179, second

impression 1619, STC 18180), and William Ames answered for the noncon-formists with two rejoinders to Morton in 1622 and 1623 respectively (STC 559 and 560, both products of the Ancient Church press, presumably under Staresmore). Ames's father-in-law, John Burgess, then revived the dispute with *An Answer Rejoyned to that Much Applauded Pamphlet of a Name-lesse Author* . . . (London, 1631) (STC 4113) and was promptly buried by Ames's "triplication" of 1633, *A Fresh Suit Against Human Ceremonies* (STC 555, Staresmore again). For Morton's *Defence* see R. C. Richardson, "Puritanism and the Ecclesiastical Authorities: the Case of the Diocese of Chester," in *Politics, Religion and the English Civil War*, ed. Brian Manning (London, 1973), pp. 13-15.

15. Nehemiah Wallington, "A Record of the Mercies of God: Or a Thankefull Remembrance," Guildhall Library, MS 204, pp. 470ff. A portion of this manuscript is reprinted in Wallington, *Historical Notices*, I:xxxvii, xliii-xlv.

16. For Lilburne's works see his *Copy of a Letter*, p. 7 and *passim*, and for other similar forms of distribution see above note 7, chap. 3; Laud, *Works*, VII:301; Greg, *A Companion to Arber*, p. 177. None of these techniques should have alarmed anyone who did not assume that the prevalent attitude towards authority of all sections of the English public was a kind of passive disobedience easily converted into active resistance.

17. For Lambe, cf. Trevor-Roper, *Laud*, pp. 152-53; Brian P. Levack, *The Civil Lawyers in England, 1603-1641* (Oxford, 1973), pp. 177-78, 246-47.

18. For Dexter see Bradford F. Swan, *Gregory Dexter of London and New England, 1610-1700* (Rochester, 1949), pp. 5-13.

19. This incident, taken from the separate interrogations of Dexter (SP 16/357, fols. 307v-309v.) and Taylor (SP 16/371, fol. 179r.), apparently forms the basis for the invention of a London press for Prynne's Tower works. The possibility is discussed in the appendix.

20. Lambe's notes on the printing trade, 14 June 1637, SP 16/361, fol. 149r.

21. Lambe's list of apprentices can be found in Greg, *Companion to Arber*, p. 333. He had no need, then, to go to the records of the Stationer's Company, but if he had done so he would have found that Gregory Dexter, son of Gregory, yeoman of Old, Northamptonshire, was apprenticed to Elizabeth Aldee for eight years, the apprenticeship to run from 3 December 1632 (just when *Histriomastix* was being completed). Taylor's apprentice-ship ran from 9 November 1630. Donald F. McKenzie, ed., *Stationers' Company Apprentices, 1605-1640* (Charlottesville, Va., 1961), p. 7. For the dating of *Histriomastix* see Greg, *Companion to Arber*, pp. 277-78.

22. Swan, *Gregory Dexter*, pp. 13-54.

23. Cf. Jones and Harris, *Pilgrim Press*, pp. 32-33, and, for a later version of the same technique, *Calendar of State Papers, Domestic Series, James I, 1623-1625*, p. 163.

24. *Acts of the Privy Council of England, 1629 May-1630 May* (London, 1960), pp. 4-5.

25. The decree is reprinted in Arber, *Transcript*, IV:528-36 (the make-work provisions are on pp. 533-34). For an analysis of the decree see Blagden, *Stationers' Company*, pp. 117-25.

26. For Heylyn and his relations with Laud see Trevor-Roper, *Laud,* pp. 82-83, 107-09.

27. Heylyn, *Cyprianus Anglicus,* pp. 210ff., 230, 296, 332; *Brief and Moderate Answer,* sigs. a3r.-v.

28. At one point in his *Briefe and Moderate Answer* to Burton (p. 34), Heylyn even managed to argue that doctrines of limited monarchy lead to *both* clerical dictatorship *and* popular uprisings: "besides in case the power of Kings were restrained by law, after the manner, that you would have it; yet should the King neglect those lawes whereby you apprehend that his power is limited, how would you helpe your selfe by this limited power? I hope you would not call a Consistorie and convent him there; or arme the people to assert their pretended liberties: though as before I said, the *Puritan tenet* is that you may doe both . . ."

29. Jacie to John Winthrop, Jr., 18 August 1637, *Winthrop Papers,* III:487. Jacie succeeded John Lothrop as the minister of the Southwark Independent church originally founded by Henry Jacob.

Notes to Chapter VII

1. John Winthrop, *The History of New England From 1630 to 1649,* ed. James Savage, 2 vols. (Boston, 1853), I:335. For other examples see E. Brooks Holifield, *The Covenant Sealed: The Development of Puritan Sacramental Theology in Old and New England, 1570-1720* (New Haven, Conn., 1974), pp. 163-64.

2. John Ball, *A Friendly Triall of the Grounds Tending to Separation* (London, 1640), preface, sig.A4r. Despite the title, "they" refers not to Brownists but to the laity who abstained from mixed communion and abjured a "stinted" liturgy: "They that break off communion in the particulars mentioned, have not proceeded to a totall separation from our congregations and assemblies, as not churches of Jesus Christ: This rigid Separation they condemn, as that which was never approved or blessed of God." Ibid., sig. Bv.

3. The most blatant instance of this tactic is Simeon Ashe and William Rathband, eds., *A Letter of Many Ministers in Old England, Requesting the Judgement of their Reverend Brethren in New England . . .* (London, 1643), sigs. A2v., a2r. This pamphlet is Thomason Tract no. E.59. (20), and was largely written by Ball in 1639 or 1640. For Ball's life and troubles see his sketch in Benjamin Brook, *The Lives of the Puritans,* 3 vols. (London, 1813), II:440-44. *A Letter* was republished the next year under a more revealing title: John Ball, *A Tryall of the New-church Way in New-England and in Old* (London, 1644).

4. For the most recent interpretation of Laud's ecclesiastical aims see Nicholas Tyacke, "Puritanism, Arminianism and Counter-Revolution," in *The Origins of the English Civil War,* ed. Conrad Russell (London, 1973), pp. 129-43.

5. For Laud at London see Seaver, *Puritan Lectureships*, pp. 254-55.

6. Laud, *Works*, VI:292. See also Trevor-Roper, *Laud*, pp. 111-13.

7. A sense of just how ordinary Laud's views on Puritans were can be gained in part by comparing his remarks in the Star Chamber to those of three distinguished members of that court in 1605 at the trial of Lewis Pickering. Sir Edward Coke, then attorney general, charged that "it was plotted by Biwater & his Complices that in there sermons & praiers they showde stirre the people to a desyre of reformacyon, which is not tollerable in a monarchie but in a Democracie . . ." Chief Justice Popham declared that "theise sorte of people would bring all to disorder & confusion, a pope in everye parishe." Lord Chancellor Ellesmere summed up for all: "The Cause of lybellinge proceedes from an inquiete & intemperate spirite, not obeyinge government; the ende is your will or else overthrowe peace of church & Common wealthe both: not uniformitie, but multiformitie." Hawarde, *Les Reportes del Cases in Camera Stellata*, pp. 224, 226, 227.

Notes to *Appendix*

1. W. J. Couper, "Was Prynne's *Newes from Ipswich* Printed in Glasgow?," *Records of the Glasgow Bibliographical Society*, VII (1923) 18-23.

2. These regulations are conveniently summarized in Walter Wilson Greg, *Some Aspects and Problems of London Publishing Between 1550 and 1650* (Oxford, 1956), chap. 1.

3. Robert Ryece to John Winthrop, 1 March 1637, *Winthrop Papers*, III:361-62; Ryece to Winthrop, ca. May 1637, ibid., p. 400.

4. See above, pp. 53, 60-61; Folke Dahl, "Amsterdam—Cradle of English Newspapers," *The Library*, 5th ser., IV (1949-50):166-78.

5. William Best's *A Just Complaint Against an Unjust Doer* is a case in point. See above n. 33, chap. 2.

6. Birch *Court and Times*, II:260.

7. Johnson "J. F. Stam," p. 186. The Stam editions are STC nos. 4134, 4142, and 20459; Johnson's "London" editions are STC nos. 4135 and 4141, and the British Library's copy of *A Divine Tragedy* bearing the shelf mark 4355.b.1 (this tract has no STC number but should be distinguished from the British Library's copy of STC 20459, which bears shelf mark 873.e.11). Johnson does not mention Prynne's *A Looking-Glasse for all Lordly Prelates* (n.p., 1636), but it also appeared in 1636 and follows exactly the typography of the "London" editions.

8. Greg, *Companion to Arber*, pp. 242-50, 253-57, 261-66, 268-74, 277, 290-91, 343-44; Arber, *Transcript of the Registers of the Company of Stationers*, III:704; IV:528, 532; R. B. McKerrow, *A Dictionary of Printers and Booksellers in England, Scotland and Ireland, and of Foreign Printers of English Books, 1557-1640* (London, 1910), pp. 51, 188.

9. The incident is discussed above, pp. 62-63.

10. Lamont, *Marginal Prynne*, p. 37.

11. See above, p. 25.

12. The confessions of Canne and Christiaans are at SP 84/154, fols. 150r.-151v., and again at SP 84/153, fol. 271r. A badly garbled version of Canne's statement was included by Benjamin Evans in *The Early English Baptists*, 2 vols. (London, 1862-64), II:108.

SELECT BIBLIOGRAPHY

THE LIST OF MANUSCRIPT collections consulted is complete. Sections II and III, however, contain only frequently cited titles, works discussed in the text, or works of particular importance to the theses of this study. Full bibliographical information for all works cited will be found at the appropriate places in the notes.

I. MANUSCRIPT SOURCES

British Library, London, England.
    Additional MSS 4275; 11, 308; 11, 764; 24, 666.
    Harleian MSS 389, 390.
    Loan 29/172.
    Sloane MSS 41; 922.
Bodleian Library, Oxford, England.
    Douce MS 173.
    Tanner MS 68.
Guildhall Library, London, England.
    MS 204.
Inner Temple Library, London, England.
    Misc. MS no. 19.

Lambeth Palace Library, London, England.
MS 943.
Public Record Office, London, England.
SP 16 (State Papers, Domestic, Charles I).
SP 84 (State Papers, Foreign, Holland).
STAC 8/19/7 (Star Chamber Records, James I).

II. Books

A. Primary

An Abridgment of that Booke Which the Ministers of Lincoln Diocess Delivered to his Majestie upon the First of December Last. N. p., 1605.

Ainsworth, Henry. *Certain Notes of M. Henry Aynsworth His Last Sermon.* Amsterdam, 1630.

Ames, William. *A Fresh Suit Against Human Ceremonies in Gods Worship.* Amsterdam, 1633.

Arber, Edward, ed. *A Transcript of the Registers of the Company of Stationers of London, 1554-1640 A.D.* 5 vols. London and Birmingham, 1875-94.

Ashe, Simeon, and Rathband, William. *A Letter of Many Ministers in Old England, Requesting the Judgement of their Reverend Brethren in New England* . . . London, 1643.

Baillie, Robert. *A Dissuasive from the Errours of the Time.* London, 1646.

————. *The Disswasive from the Errors of the Time, Vindicated From the Exceptions of Mr. Cotton and Mr. Tombes.* London, 1655.

Ball, John. *A Friendly Triall of the Grounds Tending to Separation.* London, 1640.

————. *A Tryall of the New-church Way in New-England and in Old.* London, 1644.

Bastwick, John. *The Answer of John Bastwick* . . . *to the Information of Sir John Bancks.* Leyden, 1637.

————. *A Briefe Relation of Certain Speciall and Most Materiall* . . . *Passages, and Speeches in the Starre-Chamber* . . . *at the Censure of* . . . *Dr. Bastwicke, Mr. Burton and Mr. Prynne.* Amsterdam, 1638.

————. *A Just Defence of John Bastwick Against the Calumnis of John Lilburne.* London, 1645.

————. *The Letany of John Bastwick.* Delft, 1637.

————. *The Answer of John Bastwick . . . to the Exceptions Made Against his Letany . . . This is to Follow the Letany as a Second Part Thereof.* Delft, 1637.

————. *The Vanity and Mischiefe of the Old Letany . . . This is to Follow the Letany as a Third Part of It.* Delft, 1637.

————. *A More Full Answer of John Bastwick . . . This is to Follow the Letany as a Fourth Part of It.* Delft, 1637.

————. *The Second Part of that Book Called Independency Not Gods Ordinance.* London, 1645.

Bate, Randal. *Certain Observations of that Reverend, Religious and Faithful Servant of God, . . . Mr. Randal Bate.* Amsterdam, 1624?.

Bellamie, John. *A Justification of the City Remonstrance and its Vindication.* London, 1646.

Best, William. *A Just Complaint Against an Unjust Doer.* Amsterdam, 1634.

Birch, Thomas, comp. *The Court and Times of Charles I.* Edited by R. F. Williams. 2 vols. London, 1848.

Boye, Rice. *The Importunate Beggar for Things Necessary.* Amsterdam, 1635.

————. *A Just Defence of the Importunate Beggars Importunity.* N. p., 1636.

Bradford, William. *History of Plymouth Plantation, 1620-1647.* 2 vols. Boston, 1912.

Brewer, Thomas. *Gospel Publique Worship.* London, 1656.

Burton, Henry. *An Apology of an Appeale . . . Also, an Epistle to the True-Hearted Nobility.* Amsterdam, 1636.

————. *A Divine Tragedy Lately Acted; Or a Collection of Sundry Memorable   Examples of Gods Judgements Upon Sabbath-Breakers.* Amsterdam, 1636.

————. *For God, and the King. The Summe of Two Sermons Preached on the Fifth of November . . . 1636.* Amsterdam, 1636.

————. *Israels Fast. Or, a Meditation Upon the Seventh Chapter of Joshuah.* London, 1628.

————. *A Narration of the Life of Mr. Henry Burton.* London, 1643.

————. *A Plea to an Appeale: Traversed Dialogue Wise.* London, 1626.

Canne, John. *A Necessitie of Separation From the Church of England* . . . Amsterdam, 1634.

Coke, Edward. *Les Reports de Edward Coke.* London, 1600-15.

————. *The Twelfth Part of the Reports of Sir Edward Coke, Kt.* London, 1656.

Cotton, John. *Letter of Mr. John Cotton, and Roger Williams' Reply.* Edited by Reuben A. Guild. In *The Complete Writings of Roger Williams.* Publications of the Narragansett Club, vol. I. Providence, R. I., 1866.

————. *Master John Cotton's Answer to Master Roger Williams.* Edited by J. Lewis Diman. In *The Complete Writings of Roger Williams.* Publications of the Narragansett Club, vol. II. Providence, R. I., 1867.

Culverwell, Ezekiel. *A Briefe Answer to Certain Objections Against the Treatise of Faith.* In *A Treatise of Faith.* 8th ed. London, 1646-48.

Davenport. John. *An Apologeticall Reply to a Booke Called an Answer to the Unjust Complaint of W. B.* Rotterdam, 1636.

————. *Letters of John Davenport, Puritan Divine.* Edited by Isabel MacBeath Calder. New Haven, 1937.

D'Ewes, Simonds. *The Journal of Sir Simonds D'Ewes From the Beginning of the Long Parliament to the Opening of the Trial of the Earl of Strafford.* Edited by Wallace Notestein. New Haven, 1923.

Dow, Christopher. *Innovations Unjustly Charged Upon the Present Church and State.* London, 1637.

Gardiner, Samuel Rawson, ed. *Documents Relating to the Proceedings Against W. Prynne, in 1634 and 1637.* Camden Society, n.s. vol. XVIII. London, 1877.

————. *Reports of Cases in the Courts of Star Chamber and High Commission.* Camden Society, n.s. vol. XXXIX. London, 1886.

————. *Speech of Sir R. Heath . . . in the Case of A. Leighton in the Star Chamber.* Camden Soceity, n.s. vol. XIV. London, 1875.

Goodwin, John. *Certaine Briefe Observations and Antiquaeries: on Master Prin his Twelve Questions About Church Government.* London, 1644.

Greg, Walter Wilson, ed. *A Companion to Arber.* Oxford, 1967.

Hawarde, John. *Les Reportes del Cases in Camera Stellata, 1593 to 1609.* Edited by William P. Baildon. N.p., 1894.

Hayden, Roger, ed. *The Records of a Church of Christ in Bristol, 1640-1687.* Bristol Record Society Publications, vol. XXVII. Bristol, 1974.

Heylyn, Peter. *Aerius Redivivus: Or the History of the Presbyterians . . . From the Year 1536 . . . to 1647.* Oxford, 1670.

————. *A Briefe and Moderate Answer to the Seditious and Scandalous Challenge of H. Burton.* London, 1637.

————. *Cyprianus Anglicus: Or the History of the Life and Death of . . . William . . . Archbishop of Canterbury.* London, 1668.

Hildersham, Arthur. *CVIII. Lectures Upon the Fourth of John.* London, 1632.

Howell, T. B., ed. *Cobbett's Complete Collection of State Trials and Proceedings for High Treason and Other Crimes and Midemeanours From the Earliest Period to the Present Time.* 33 vols. London, 1809-28.

Hudson, William. *A Treatise of the Star Chamber.* In *Collectanea Juridica.* Edited by Francis Hargrave. 2 vols. London, 1791-92.

King Charles his Defence Against Some Trayterous Observations Upon King James his Judgement of a King and of a Tyrant. London, 1642.

Laud, William. *The Works of the Most Reverend Father in God, William Laud.* Edited by W. Scott and J. Bliss. 7 vols. in 9. Oxford, 1847-60.

Leighton, Alexander. *An Appeal to the Parliament, Or Sions Plea Against the Prelacie.* Amsterdam, 1628 [i.e., 1629].

————. *An Epitome or Briefe Discoverie . . . of the . . . Great Troubles that Dr. Leighton Suffered in his Body, Estate, and Family.* London, 1646.

————. *A Friendly Triall of the Treatise of Faith.* Amsterdam, 1624.

————? *King James his Judgement of a King and of a Tyrant.* London, 1642.

————. *A Shorte Treatise Against Stage-Playes.* Amsterdam, 1625.

————. *Speculum Belli Sacri; Or the Looking-Glasse of the Holy War.* Amsterdam, 1624.

Lilburne, John. *The Christian Mans Triall: Or a True Relation of the First Apprehension and Severall Examinations of John Lilburne.* London, 1641.

————. *A Copy of a letter Written by J. Lilburne . . . to J. Ingram and H. Hopkins.* N.p., 1640?

————. *A Worke of the Beast, Or a Relation of a Most Unchristian Censure, Executed Upon J. Lilburne.* Amsterdam, 1638.

Moxon, Joseph. *Mechanick Exercises on the Whole Art of Printing, 1683-4.* Edited by Herbert Davis and Harry Carter. 2d ed. London, 1962.

Paget, John. *An Answer to the Unjust Complaints of William Best . . .* Amsterdam, 1635.

Price, John. *The City Remonstrance Remonstrated, or an Answer to Colonell J. Bellamy.* London, 1646.

Prynne, William. *The Antipathie of the English Prelacie, Both to Regall Monarchy, and Civil Unity.* London, 1641.

————. *A Catalogue of Such Testimonies in all Ages as Plainly Evidence Bishops and Presbyters To Be One . . .* The Netherlands, 1637.

————. *A Catalogue of Such Testimonies in all Ages as Plainly Evidence Bishops and Presbyters To Be One . . .* 2d ed. N.p., 1641?

————. *Certaine Quaeres Propounded to Bowers at the Name of Jesus . . .* Amsterdam, 1636.

————. *A Full Reply to Certain Brief Observations.* London, 1644.

————. *Histriomastix, The Players Scourge.* London, 1633.

————. *A Looking-Glasse for all Lordly Prelates.* N.p., 1636.

————. *The Lords Day, the Sabbath Day. Or, a Briefe Answer to . . . a Late Treatise of the Sabbath-Day . . .* 2d ed., much enlarged. Amsterdam, 1636.

————. *The Lyar Confounded: Or, a Briefe Refutation of John Lilburne's . . . Case.* London, 1645.

————. *A New Discovery of the Prelates Tyrrany in their Late Prosecutions of Mr. W. Pryn, . . . Dr. John Bastwick . . . and Mr. H. Burton.* London, 1641.

————? *Newes from Ipswich.* N.p., 1636.

————. *A Quench-Coale. Or, a Briefe . . . Inquirie in What Place . . . the Lords-Table Ought to be Situated.* Amsterdam, 1637.

————. *The Unbishoping of Timothy and Titus.* Amsterdam, 1636.

Robinson, John. *The Works of John Robinson*. Edited by Robert Ashton. 3 vols. London, 1851.

Rushworth, John. *Historical Collections of Private Passages of State, Weighty Matters in Law, Remarkable Proceedings* . . . 8 vols. London, 1721-22.

S., B. *Innocency Cleared* . . . *in a Letter Sent to Mr. H. Burton* . . . *in Defence of Dr. Bastwick*. London, 1645.

Smectymnuus [pseud]. *A Vindication of the Answer to the Humble Remonstrance*. London, 1641.

Sparke, Michael. *A Catalogue of Printed Books Written by W. Prynne* . . . London, 1643.

Staresmore, Sabine. *The Unlawfulnes of Reading in Prayer*. Amsterdam, 1619.

Stearns, Raymond P., ed. *Letters and Documents by or Relating to Hugh Peter*. Salem, Mass., 1935.

T., A. *A Christian Reprofe Against Contention*. Amsterdam, 1631.

Wallington, Nehemiah. *Historical Notices of Events . . . in the Reign of Charles I*. Edited by R. Webb. 2 vols. London, 1864.

White, Francis. *A Treatise of the Sabbath-Day*. London, 1635.

Wickens, Nathaniel [William Prynne?]. *Wood Street-Compters Plea for its Prisoner*. Amsterdam, 1638.

Widdowes, Giles. *The Lawlesse Kneelesse Schismaticall Puritan*. Oxford, 1631.

Williams, John. Annotated copy of William Laud, *A Speech Delivered in the Starr-Chamber* . . . London, 1788.

The Winthrop Papers. Edited by the Massachusetts Historical Society. Boston, 1929.

à Wood, Anthony. *The Life and Times of Anthony Wood, Antiquary, at Oxford, 1632-1695, Described by Himself*. Edited by Andrew Clark. 5 vols. Oxford, 1891-1900.

B. *Secondary*

Bennett, H. S. *English Books and Readers, 1603-1640: Being a Study in the History of the Book Trade in the Reigns of James I and Charles I*. Cambridge, 1970.

Blagden, Cyprian. *The Stationers' Company: A History, 1403-1959*. London, 1960.

Burrage, Champlin. *The Early English Dissenters in the Light of Recent Research (1550-1641)*. Cambridge, 1912.

Collinson, Patrick. *The Elizabethan Puritan Movement.* Berkeley, 1967.

―――. "Towards a Broader Understanding of the Early Dissenting Tradition." In *The Dissenting Tradition: Essays for Leland H. Carlson.* Edited by C. Robert Cole and Michael E. Moody. Athens, Ohio, 1974.

Davies, Horton. *Worship and Theology in England from Andrewes to Baxter and Fox, 1603-1690.* Princeton, 1975.

Gardiner, Samuel Rawson. *History of England from the Accession of James I to the Outbreak of the Civil War, 1603-1642.* 10 vols. London, 1884-86.

Greg, Walter Wilson. *Some Aspects and Problems of London Publishing Between 1550 and 1650.* Oxford, 1956.

Gregg, Pauline. *Free-Born John: A Biography of John Lilburne.* London, 1961.

Haller, William. *The Rise of Puritanism.* New York, 1938.

Harris, J. Rendel, and Jones, Stephen K. *The Pilgrim Press: A Bibliographical and Historical Memorial of the Books Printed at Leyden by the Pilgrim Fathers.* Cambridge, 1922.

Hawkins, Michael. "The Government: Its Role and Its Aims." In *The Origins of the English Civil War.* Edited by Conrad Russell. London, 1973.

Hill, Christopher. *Antichrist in Seventeenth-Century England.* London, 1971.

―――. "The Many-Headed Monster in Late Tudor and Early Stuart Political Thinking." In *From the Renaissance to the Counter Reformation: Essays in Honour of Garrett Mattingly.* Edited by Charles H. Carter. New York, 1965.

Kleerkooper, M.M. *De Boekhandel te Amsterdam, Voornamelijk in de 17e Eeuw.* 2 vols. 's-Gravenhage, 1914-16.

Lamont, William. *Godly Rule: Politics and Religion, 1603-1660.* London, 1969.

―――. *Marginal Prynne, 1600-1669.* London, 1963.

McKenzie, Donald F., ed. *Stationers' Company Apprentices, 1605-1640.* Charlottesville, Va., 1961.

McKerrow, R. B. *A Dictionary of Printers and Booksellers in England, Scotland and Ireland, and of Foreign Printers of English Books, 1557-1640.* London, 1910.

Miller, Perry. *Orthodoxy in Massachusetts, 1630-50; A Genetic Study.* Cambridge, Mass., 1933.

Nuttall, Geoffrey F. *Visible Saints: The Congregational Way, 1640-1660*. Oxford, 1957.

Pearl, Valerie. *London and the Outbreak of the Puritan Revolution: City Government and National Politics, 1625-43*. London, 1961.

Plooij, Daniel. *The Pilgrim Fathers from a Dutch Point of View*. New York, 1932.

Richardson, R. C. *Puritanism in North-West England: A Regional Study of the Diocese of Chester*. Manchester, 1972.

Rostenberg, Leona. *The Minority Press and the English Crown: A Study in Repression, 1558-1625*. Nieuwkoop [The Netherlands], 1971.

Seaver, Paul S. *The Puritan Lectureships: The Politics of Religious Dissent, 1560-1662*. Stanford, 1970.

Sprunger, Keith L. *The Learned Doctor William Ames: Dutch Backgrounds of English and American Puritanism*. Urbana, Ill., 1972.

Stearns, Raymond P. *Congregationalism in The Dutch Netherlands: The Rise and Fall of the English Congregational Classis, 1621-1635*. Chicago, 1940.

————. *The Strenuous Puritan: Hugh Peters. 1598-1660*. Urbana, Ill., 1954.

Swan, Bradford F. *Gregory Dexter of London and New England, 1610-1700*. Rochester, 1949.

Trevor-Roper, H. R. *Archbishop Laud, 1573-1645*. 2d ed. London, 1963.

Tyacke, Nicholas, "Puritanism, Arminianism and Counter-Revolution." In *The Origins of the English Civil War*. Edited by Conrad Russell. London, 1973.

Usher, Roland G. *The Rise and Fall of the High Commission*. Oxford, 1913.

White, B. R. *The English Separatist Tradition: From the Marian Martyrs to the Pilgrim Fathers*. Oxford, 1971.

III. Periodicals and Other

Adams, S. L. "Captain Thomas Gainsford, the 'Vox Spiritus' and the *Vox Populi*." *Bulletin of the Institute of Historical Research* XLIX (1976):141-44.

Bryant, Jerry H. "John Reynolds of Exeter and his Canon: A Footnote." *The Library*. 5th ser. XVIII (1963):299-303.

Collinson, Patrick. "The Godly: Aspects of Popular Protestantism in Elizabethan England." Paper delivered at the *Past and Present* Conference on Popular Religion. London, 1966. Xeroxed.

Couper, W. J. "Was Prynne's *Newes from Ipswich* Printed in Glasgow?" *Records of the Glasgow Bibliographical Society* VII (1923):18-23.

Curtis, Mark H. "William Jones: Puritan Printer and Propagandist." *The Library*. 5th ser. XIX (1964):38-66.

Dahl, Folke. "Amsterdam—Cradle of English Newspapers." *The Library*. 5th ser. IV (1949-50):166-78.

Johnson, A. F. "The Exiled English Church at Amsterdam and its Press." *The Library*. 5th ser. V (1950-51):219-42.

————. "J. F. Stam, Amsterdam, and English Bibles." *The Library*. 5th ser. IX (1954):185-93.

————. "Willem Christiaans, Leyden and his English Books." *The Library*. 5th ser. X (1955):121-23.

Phillips, Henry E. I. "The Last Years of the Court of Star Chamber, 1630-41." *Transactions of the Royal Historical Society*. 4th ser. XXI (1939):103-31.

Sprunger, Keith L. "Other Pilgrims in Leiden: Hugh Goodyear and the English Reformed Church." *Church History* XLI (1972):46-60.

Wiener, Carol Z. "The Beleaguered Isle. A Study of Elizabethan and Early Jacobean Anti-Catholicism." *Past and Present* LI (1971): 27-62.

Wilson, J. Dover. "Richard Schilders and the English Puitans." *Transactions of the Bibliographical Society* XI (1909-11):65-134.

Wright, Louis B. "Propaganda Against James I's 'Appeasement' of Spain." *Huntington Library Quarterly* VI (1942-43):149-72.

INDEX